MITCHELL BEAZLEY
DISCOVERING WINE COUNTRY

Tuscany

Monty Waldin

D0916591

Series editor: Patrick Matthews

DISCOVERING WINE COUNTRY
TUSCANY
by Monty Waldin

First published in Great Britain in 2006
by Mitchell Beazley, an imprint of Octopus Publishing Group Ltd,
2–4 Heron Quays, London E14 4JP.

A CIP catalogue record for this book is available from the British Library.

ISBN: 1 84533 171 0

The author and publishers will be grateful for any information which will assist them in keeping future editions up to date. Although all reasonable care has been taken in the preparation of this book, neither the publishers nor the author can accept any liability for any consequences arising from the use thereof, or the information contained therein.

Photographs by Victoria McTernan
Map creation by Encompass Graphics

Commissioning Editor Hilary Lumsden
Executive Art Editor Yasia Williams-Leedham
Managing Editor Julie Sheppard
Editor Emma Rice
Designer Gaelle Lochner
Index Hilary Bird
Production Gary Hayes

Typeset in Futura and Sabon

Printed and bound by Toppan Printing Company in China

Contents

How to use this book

Discovering Wine Country is all about getting you from the page to the producer. Each chapter covers a specific winemaking region of interest, and includes a map of the area featured, with places of interest marked using the symbols below. The leading wine producers mentioned are all given a map grid reference so you can see exactly where they are.

The maps include key features to help you navigate your way round the routes, but they are not intended to replace detailed road maps, or indeed detailed vineyard maps, normally available from local tourist offices or the local wine bureau (*see* below, right).

It wouldn't be practical to mark each and every grower on the maps. Instead the sign ❖ means that an area or village is home to at least one recommended wine producer. The wine regions covered are packed with other points of interest for the wine enthusiast that are unrelated to actual wine purchasing. These are shown as ⛪ Sometimes this includes growers who don't sell direct but whose status is such that they will be on any wine lover's itinerary. Recommended restaurants are marked ⫶O⫶ and towns and villages where there's a tourist office are marked ⓘ, which is especially useful for finding B&Bs and campsites.

Quick reference map symbols
❖   recommended wine producer
⛪   wine tourist site
★   tourist attraction
⫶O⫶   recommended restaurant
ⓘ   tourist information centre

▭   named wine region

═══   author's suggested wine route(s) to follow, with information about how long the route is and any other useful tips

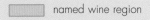   scale bar

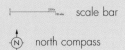   north compass

Boxed information
▭   the contact details of hotels, restaurants, tourist information, hire shops, transport facilities, and other points of interest.

▭   wine related information as well as the author's selection of the top growers to visit in the specific area featured, including contact details and a map reference.

Local wine bureaus:

www.chianticlassico.com

www.collisenesi.it

www.vernaccia.com

www.consorziobrunellodimontalcino.it

www.vinonobiledimontalcino.it

www.lastradadelvino.com

www.collimaremma.it

Introduction

It is pretty safe to assume that Tuscany would appear on almost everyone's wish list of top ten wine regions when thinking about tending that retirement vineyard in the sun.

Living the dream

The timeless landscape, the Mediterranean coast, and its climate, not to mention the renowned and healthy diet, make Tuscany the perfect location for Planet Wine's lifestyle generation even before you consider that the region's has a history of winemaking stretching back thousands of years.

For most of us, the added bonus would be the access Tuscany provides to some of the world's greatest cultural treasures: the Uffizi museum in Florence, UNESCO world heritage sites like San Gimignano, and the annual *Palio* in Siena.

But for others, Tuscany particularly, and Italy in general, remains a place where people's perspective on wine remains reassuringly, almost stubbornly, down to earth.

Wine is still something to be enjoyed at table, one element of the dining experience, with no more or less import than the contents of the bread basket or the olive oil cruet.

For sure, wine in Italy is a catalyst for conversation, but as often as not it remains just that, rather than an end in itself to be talked about for hours, *ad nauseam*, as can be the case in Bordeaux or Champagne, for example. You don't get "wine dinners" in Tuscany, but you do get dinners with wine.

Perhaps this is why Tuscan wine cellars are functional buildings where the business of winemaking has been carried out by successive generations, each one adding its personal, invariably imaginative touch.

From a professional standpoint, this creativity in Tuscany always seems to provide you with something new to discover, be it a way of growing the grapes up trees – a modern copy of the method used by the Etruscans who first settled Tuscany 2,000 years ago – or of winemaking, such as removing the pips from the red wine vats as early as possible during fermentation to prevent the wines becoming too bitter.

BELOW *The caffès of Siena's beautiful Piazza del Campo.*

And there are always new producers to discover, too. In historically famous regions like Chianti and its better sub-zones like Colline Lucchesi, grapes from vineyards previously used by cooperatives are being bottled by single estates; plus there is a new wave of plantings in emerging regions, such as Morellino di Scansano in Grosseto province or along the Etruscan coast where the once one-vineyard-wonder Bolgheri zone (for Sassicaia) is now competing with Val di Cornia and Montescudaio, not to mention a slew of new Bolgheri estates.

ABOVE *The fairytale landscape of Tuscany is endlessly bewitching at any time of day.*

Improving on the old

Siena's Piazza del Campo hasn't changed much since I was last there as a student tourist in 1986, with many of the *caffès* still under the same ownership. But Tuscan wine has: it is more confident now, thanks less to trickery in the cellar and more to a renewed vigour in the vineyards, notably with better vinestocks of Tuscany's signature grape, Sangiovese, which have been widely planted over the last 20 years.

And this brings us back to where we began, at table, for Sangiovese is the most food-friendly of grapes, tempting you with its black and red fruit smell, teasing you with its bittersweet taste, and its prickly impression on the tongue. For although Tuscany has a blockbuster reputation as a tourist destination, blockbuster wines do not reign supreme, as they seem to do in Bordeaux or California. Sangiovese is just not suited to the blockbuster style. Worth bearing in mind should your week in the Tuscan sun become your retirement occupation.

Understanding
Tuscany

	Chianti Rufina and Pomino	Arezzo (Colli Aretini)
	Florence (Chianti Colli Fiorentini) and Montespertoli	Montalcino
	Pisa (Chianti Colline Pisane)	Montepulciano and Val d'Orcia
	Chianti Classico	The Etruscan coast
	San Gimignano	Grosseto
	Siena (Chianti Colli Senesi)	Lucca, Carmignano, and northwest Tuscany

Why Tuscany makes great wines

If you asked the world's most famous vineyard regions to walk down the catwalk like supermodels, the appearance of Tuscany would get the photographers snapping the most eagerly of all. While Bordeaux has beautiful towns like St-Emilion, it is unremittingly flat to the eye; Champagne's white chalk soils are eyecatching but in an austere way; and Napa Valley's name is arguably more romantic sounding than the reality, unless burger bars and tourist-filled pick-ups stacked nose-to-tail on Highway 29 during summer are your idea of fun.

Beauty is more than skin deep

Looks aside, though, what all great wine regions do have in common is that they are able to make great wine in the vineyard, rather than in the winery. As the old adage goes, while you can make a poor wine from great grapes, you'll never make a great wine from poor grapes.

What makes Tuscany so special is that it has generally very fine topsoils that allow the vines' roots easy passage into the firm sub-soils, releasing nutrients and water to vines slowly, so they don't get lazy and produce big grapes with little flavour rather than small grapes with lots of flavour. The Mediterranean climate provides plenty of sun in summer, cold temperatures in

BELOW An impressive hilltop wine estate looking out over its vineyards.

winter to allow the vines a much-needed period of rest (or dormancy), and just enough rain in late summer to allow the vines a final drink as they begin switching their energies from growing leaves and shoots to ripening the grape pulp for sugars (potential alcohol) and the skins for colour and flavour.

Going organic

An increasing number of winemakers, consumers, and critics are realizing that "less is more", meaning that the fewer treatments such as sprays and fertilizers are needed in the vineyard, the better the wine will be. Tuscany's dry. sunny summer climate is perfect for organic vine-growing – fungal diseases like rot and mildew, the bane of organic producers elsewhere, are both easily controlled here using organic methods.

ABOVE *Demi-johns for transporting wine back home from the winery.*

In fact, Tuscany has the highest percentage of organic vineyards in Italy, the world's biggest organic wine-producing country, and ranks with the ultra-green Alsace as the world's most environmentally friendly wine-growing region. Perhaps this is why it has attracted so many "lifestyle" winemakers, from Germany, Switzerland, and the UK, all looking to live *"la dolce vita"*, making great wines in as natural a way as possible.

As autumns are usually dry, with rain coming in short bursts, winemakers can wait as long as possible for the grapes to ripen fully, super-important with the somewhat tricky Sangiovese being the main red wine grape. Pick it too early and the wines will taste nice and fresh, but also a tad green, too.

Modern traditions

Where other decisions need to be made by the winemakers, the Tuscans can draw on 2,500 years of wine-growing experience, starting with their ancestors the Etruscans, who introduced vines and olive trees to the area from the 8th century BC. They found that growing the vines a bit higher off the ground than the Ancient Greeks did made for better wine, and even today most Tuscan vineyards are at what is called mid-height – neither touching the ground nor as high as a normal olive tree.

And you only have to look at how well the private gardens or public parks in Tuscany are kept to realize that the people here feel comfortable working on and living off the land. They have retained their tremendous expertise in farming, too, be it for cereal crops, olives, or vines. The Pisa and Florence universities, both hotbeds of viticultural research, are ensuring that traditional knowledge and skills can be passed on to the new generation, in order to keep Tuscany at the forefront of Italian wine.

FACTS AND FIGURES

Tuscany has nearly **70,000 hectares of vines,** which is roughly 10% of Italy's total vineyard area. There are around **140,000 farms with vines,** but about 40% sell their grapes to cooperatives and merchants rather than making their own wine. **Tuscany produces 2.5 million hectolitres or 330 million bottles of wine** in a national total of 50–60 million hectolitres (**Italy is the largest wine producer in the world**). Of this, 91% is red, 8% is dry white, and 1% is sparkling and sweet white wine. **Less than 40% of this wine is sold in Italy,** with the biggest foreign markets being the USA, the UK, Germany, the Netherlands, Belgium, and Luxembourg – with Asia also rapidly becoming more important.

The people

S oil and climate are crucial for wine, but we should always remember the people behind the wines, too. Around 140,000 Tuscan businesses are involved in the production, packaging, sale, or promotion of wine, and one-third of the Tuscan economy is driven by agriculture, wine, and, increasingly, wine and farm tourism (or *agriturismo* in Italian).

BELOW *Fresh local produce delivered to your door.*

A family affair

In Tuscany, you'll be hard pressed to find a Tuscan – and there are 3.5 million people living in the region – with absolutely no involvement in wine. And despite a move away from the land, sparked by the growth of cities from the 1950s, even Tuscans who no longer live in the country will leave town at weekends to spend time with their extended families who, as well as a vegetable patch, will invariably have a row or two of vines, too.

Tuscany gets its name from the Etruscans, a mysterious people who settled here after the Bronze Age. No one knows where they came from but they were superbly organized, developing industries like mining and agriculture, and founding self-governing city-states like Volterra, Cortona, and Arezzo.

Even today, Tuscan people still identify themselves more with their local town – Siena, Florence, Montalcino – than with the Tuscany region or on a national level with Italy, not surprising when you consider city-states like Siena and Florence fought constantly during the Middle Ages like mini-countries, and that Italy became a nation state only as recently as 1861.

Independent creativity

The most traditional Tuscan towns like Siena and Montalcino are still subdivided into *contrade* or wards, and inhabitants still dress up in the colours of their *contrade* to compete against each other during traditional competitions like archery in Montalcino or horse-riding in Siena during the *Palio*.

Tuscans are nothing if not creative. Florence's financial and trading power gave its emerging class of wealthy businessmen, like the Medicis, the chance to show off their wealth by patronizing the arts. Poets like Dante, Petrarca, and Boccaccio refused to use the Latin of the Church, creating the modern Italian language (even today Tuscan is considered "standard Italian"); and local painters like Botticelli, Michelangelo, and Leonardo da Vinci emerged to spur the medieval *Risorgimento* – the renaissance or rebirth of cultural values like art, sculpture, and theatre that brought an end to the Dark Ages.

It is perhaps no surprise then, with creativity bursting from every pore, that Tuscany's wine producers forged the modern re-birth of Italian wine in the 1970s and 1980s, subverting wine laws to create Super Tuscans, innovatively labelled and blended wines that achieve higher prices than historic wines like Chianti and Brunello.

Bean counting

Tuscans are superstitious; don't be surprised if your cellar tour guide prefers to pass under the edge of an archway rather than through the middle to avoid bad luck. They are more reserved than their neighbours in Liguria and Lazio (Rome); and they are ridiculed by their Italian peers for living on a diet dominated by beans: hence their nickname *mangiafagioli* or bean eaters.

Tuscans also have a reputation for being careful with money. The powerful bank, Monte dei Paschi di Siena, is based here, a legacy of Siena's domination of Florence in the banking world from the late 15th century. Don't expect a favourable response to the question "Can I have a discount on this wine?"

Since World War II Tuscan agriculture has been in a state of flux. The Socialist-inspired upheavals of the 1960s saw large landholdings broken up with the end of the *mezzadria* or share-cropping system, liberating peasants from their landlords, but also exposing them to market forces they ill understood.

A wave of rash vineyard plantings – the Great Historical Error – saw Tuscany saddled with a reputation for poor quality. Many peasants sold up to banks, insurance companies, wealthy Milanese, English ex-pats (who coined the phrase "Chiantishire"), businessmen from Piedmont, and "well-connected" investors from Naples and Sicily.

Naturally suspicious of foreigners, Tuscans seem to welcome foreign money more than those who provide it. However, once investors show their commitment, they soon become part of the community. Tuscans realize only too well that they are fortunate to live in one of Europe's most beautiful landscapes, and they know how to maximize this. Money generated by tourism maintains historic treasures and keeps the landscape alive. Hence foreign visitors are welcomed, especially those who spend. Younger Italians have a good grasp of foreign languages, even if they prefer you to try to speak what they consider to be the world's most beautiful language, their own.

ABOVE *Seasonal fruits and vegetables – grown on individual plots – make up a large part of the Tuscan diet.*

Seasons and festivals

S pending all your time inside in wine cellars may mean you miss out on the fun of getting out into the vineyards. The only time when absolutely nothing is going on in the vines is just after harvest, usually September to October. By November, once most of the leaves have fallen, pruning begins. The vine is cut back to control the size of the following year's crop and to stop the vineyard becoming a jungle. Pruning of the vines can continue all through winter, but must be completed by spring.

Following the seasons

Tuscany's olive trees are pruned later than the vines, because the olives are sometimes picked as late as November or December. One of the most atmospheric sights is to see smoke swirling slowly in the winter air as the vine and olive prunings are burnt, with grey smoke rising from the deciduous vine prunings and creamy yellow smoke from the evergreen olive.

In spring, as the soil warms up, the vine buds burst, and new green shoots start growing. By late April these shoots are high enough to need to be tied to supporting wires.

In May and June the vines flower. A period of dry, fine, and not-too-windy weather will ensure a good fruit-set. The earth between the vine rows will spring back to life, with flowers, clovers, and grasses appearing, and the scrub around the vineyards in dry areas like Elba will become a carpet of colour.

The time between flowering and harvest is roughly three and four months, with picking earliest in the warmest zones like Elba, Arezzo, and along the Etruscan coast.

However, it is only during August that the small, hard, green berries begin to swell, soften, and change colour – to golden yellow in the case of white varieties and dark purple in the case of reds.

The first two weeks of August are the worst time to visit wineries, as very few proprietors will be there. This is the most popular fortnight in the Italian calendar for annual holidays. Things get back to normal by the beginning of September when wineries become a flurry of activity.

Bottling often takes place now, to empty the vats of last year's crop ready for the new intake. Presses, pumps, and hoses need to be cleaned; new barrels need to be ordered and arranged; food – and the inevitable paperwork – organized for an army of pickers; machine harvesters (where used) dusted down and checked.

BELOW *Italy's Catholic heritage is a constant feature.*

Once harvest starts, it can be difficult to arrange winery visits. Many estates will stop giving guided tours, but will still be open for wine tasting and sales.

ABOVE *Three of the grape varieties used in Tuscany are Sangiovese, Trebbiano, and Canaiolo.*

When to visit

Tuscany's Mediterranean climate means winters are usually never bitingly cold, but snow is very common on the higher ground; and Tuscan agritourism farmhouses are often more geared to keep you cool in summer than cosy in winter. The sunniest months are June, July, and August, with July and August the hottest; but you can wander around in just a light shirt from April onwards. Even as the days shorten in autumn Tuscany is not particularly damp or humid, but expect heavy if short bursts of rain from November to March. For local weather updates and predictions see the website that the wine-growers use: www2.arsia.toscana.it/meteo.

Local festivals

Village festivals are still very much a part of Tuscan life. There are hundreds annually, usually revolving around local food: truffles in the Orcia Valley, chestnuts on Monte Amiata, fish on the Etruscan coast, beef in the Chiana Valley. The Tuscan authorities publish a free list of festivals and fairs called *Sagre e Fiere,* which you can download from the website www.regione.toscana.it or pick up a free copy from any tourist office.

Knowing the wines

I talian wines in general and Tuscan wines in particular have a reputation for bamboozling even the most well-read wine experts. Walking down the Tuscan section of a supermarket aisle can feel like being surrounded by inner-city graffiti, with words and colours seemingly just a meaningless code understood only by a select few.

Making sense of it

The profusion of labels, grapes, and regions of origin, not to mention white wine styles ranging from bone dry to incredibly sweet, red wines of every shade or colour between light ruby to deep blackcurrant, plus sparkling wines that can be either frothily sweet and inconsequential or dry with finer, more serious bubbles, makes our collective incomprehension understandable.

As a generalization you'll find the secret to success in buying Tuscan wine is to ignore everything on the label except the name of the producer. When you have found the name of a producer you can trust, then see what else is on offer in terms of colour, sweetness, and style: red or white, sweet or dry, still or sparkling.

BELOW *A confusing array of labels faces the consumer.*

Beyond the label

Don't assume that a VDT (*vino da tavola*) wine, supposedly at the bottom of the quality scale, is always necessarily inferior to a DOCG (*denominazione di origine controllata e garantita*) wine, from what is supposed to be the top. It might be better or worse, as a comparison between a cheap Vino Nobile di Montepulciano DOCG and a classy *vino da tavola rosso* from the Chianti Classico zone or the Etruscan coast will show.

This is because historically the VDT designation offered more sensible rules on blending (and the possibility of higher yields) than those for Tuscany's most historic wine, Chianti, in the days when Chianti's rule-makers forced producers to blend white grapes into their red wines (from the late 1800s until 1995). Quality-conscious producers who wanted to make red wines from nothing but red wine grapes opted for the basic VDT designation for their best blends, creating what became known as the Super Tuscans: high-priced wines labelled ostensibly as plonk.

Tuscany produces about 2.5 million hectolitres (330 million bottles) of wine annually, around 5% of the national total. The vast majority of Tuscan wine is red (about 90%) and most Tuscan red wines are made mainly from the Sangiovese grape. The best Sangiovese wines have crisp, dry, fruity-floral flavours of irises, violets, and bitter red cherries and a moderate but never particularly deep colour.

Native to Italy, Sangiovese is probably descended from an ancient wild crossing of a red Tuscan grape called Ciliegiolo and an obscure southern Mediterranean red grape called Montenuovo. Over time, many different strains of Sangiovese have evolved. The best have smallish berries giving wines of good colour and are called Brunello in Montalcino, Prugnolo in Montepulciano, Morellino in Scansano, and Sangiovese Grosso everywhere else. A poor strain of Sangiovese called Sangiovese di Romagna, which was used heavily for replanting in the 1960s and 1970s, gives high yields but lacks quality and is gradually being weeded out of Tuscan vineyards.

Red wines that are supposed to be made from 100% Sangiovese include Brunello di Montalcino DOCG, Rosso di Montalcino DOC, Vino Nobile di Montepulciano DOCG, and Morellino di Scansano DOC. But some examples taste as if other grapes have been blended in to sex up Sangiovese – Cabernet heightens Sangiovese's black fruit character and boosts colour, Merlot rounds out its bitter tannins, while Syrah softens its spiky core. If badly grown and picked too early Sangiovese can be a bit dry, bitter, tannic, colourless, and thin.

Distinguished Chianti

Chianti and Chianti Classico DOCG wines are made from a minimum 85% Sangiovese. Chianti is the most famous red wine name in Italy, but Chianti and its various sub-zones around

LABEL LORE

In Italy there are so many often contradictory and overlapping laws, and furthermore so many of them are badly policed and widely flouted for both the best of creative intentions as well as more sinister reasons. You should never worry whether a wine is labelled as merely table wine (***vino da tavola* or VDT**), or with a geographical indication of origin (***indicazione geografica tipica* or IGT**), a controlled region of origin (***denominazione di origine controllata* or DOC**) or even from a controlled region of origin with guarantee (***denominazione di origine controllata e garantita* or DOCG**).

BELOW *A quintessential Tuscan view of cypress and terracotta.*

Lucca, Pisa, Montespertoli, Montalbano, Arezzo, Florence, Siena, and Rufina remain among the most confusing wines to get to grips with, despite the Chianti producers spending millions of euros on vineyard research, rebranding, and redefining the rules on winemaking and blending.

Chiantis labelled as "Chianti Classico" from the historic heart of the Chianti zone should taste smoother and fuller than those labelled just "Chianti", but quite often they don't.

At the cheaper end of the scale there can be little obvious difference between a red wine labelled Chianti and one labelled Chianti Classico. Chianti Classico is supposed to come from much better vineyard sites than Chianti, but of course the Chianti Classico boundaries include some of the worst vineyard land in Tuscany.

In one case the Chianti Classico boundary appears to have been extended to include the huge vineyards surrounding the main winery (more like a factory in reality) of a powerful Tuscan merchant. The soils here are far too heavy to produce wine worthy of "Classico" designation – but somehow they got in…

Name is no guarantee

So, while it is true that most Chianti Classico tastes better than most Chianti, it is not always the case, and the premium you pay for the Classico name is not justified often enough – even though the *e garantita* part of the DOCG means wines should undergo a rigorous taste test to ensure they really are up to par. And the word *riserva* where used on any DOC/G wine is no guarantee of extra quality either – it just means the wine has been aged in wood a bit longer than the *normale*, and will have a touch more alcohol.

BELOW *A Tuscan estate surrounded by its vines – a retirement dream for many.*

It's no surprise that the best Chianti sub-zones like Rufina are trying to break away from Chianti; while growers in Chianti Colline Pisane are dumping the Chianti name in favour of a "Terre di Pisa" designation for their reds, arguing that Chianti has become a meaningless term.

One bright recent move was the creation of catch-all IGT designations for red, white, and pink Tuscan wines. These allow 100% varietal labelling, for example 100% Chardonnay whites, or 100% Sangiovese or 100% Merlot reds. But they also allow Tuscan and non-Tuscan grapes to be blended together, which gives growers flexibility. IGT Toscana Rossos can be among the most exciting wines in Tuscany, and although some achieve very high prices, usually for wines with fantasy names aged in expensive new oak barrels and sold in the heaviest and tallest bottles money can buy, many others in less pretentious packaging offer great value drinking.

However, the Chianti producers undid all that good work, in outlawing the blending in of white grapes, by short-sightedly allowing foreign (and usually French) grapes like Merlot, Syrah, and Cabernet in with the Sangiovese, Canaiolo, Ciliegiolo, and Colorino into Chianti. So wines labelled Chianti or Chianti Classico and IGT Toscana Rossos from the Chianti zones began to taste remarkably similar to one another.

Losing identity

It would make more sense if anything labelled Chianti could come only from Tuscan or Italian grapes (Sangiovese for elegance, Canaiolo for aroma and texture, Colorino for structure, Ciliegiolo for seasoning, even Malvasia Nera for exoticism), leaving IGT and VDT wines to be blended from everything else. Then Chiantis would taste Italian and the IGT wines would taste more international in style. But that, of course, would be too simple.

So when you buy a Chianti you have no guarantee whether it will taste like a red Bordeaux (from up to 15% Merlot and Cabernet having been blended with the Sangiovese), a red Rhône (if up to 15% Syrah has been used), or like Tuscan wine should taste if made only with native grape varieties.

So, if you care that your Chianti or Chianti Classico tastes like it should, look for the name of the producer above all else. Wines like Pomino (from within the Chianti Rufina zone) and Carmignano, which have always allowed Sangiovese/ Cabernet blends, have an established, and clearly defined, track record dating back, in Carmignano's case, to the 19th century and beyond.

So, too, do the red wines of the Tuscan coast or Etruscan coast, where you can pick up clear differences between the wines moving north to south from Montescudaio, Bolgheri, Val di Cornia, and the island of Elba, with the red wine flavours becoming softer, warmer, and riper the further south you go. These wines tend to be softer than Chianti anyway, as they are more Mediterranean-influenced, and percentages of "other" grapes are more generous than for Chianti. Bolgheri, for example, made its name with Cabernet Sauvignon-dominated reds like Sassicaia and Ornellaia from the early 1970s.

Tuscany's trendy areas at the moment are Bolgheri on the Etruscan coast, which has seen waves of new vineyard planting in the last few years, and Scansano in Grosseto province, which has seen a stampede of producers from further north planting Sangiovese, known there as Morellino. A wealth of young vines in both Bolgheri and Scansano means the jury is still out on the potential of these newer vineyard areas as growers feel their way stylistically.

New varieties and regions

The most underrated region of Tuscany is probably Colline Lucchesi (its neighbour Montecarlo has yet to fulfil its potential), which has warm daytime sun to get grapes ripe, night cooling to keep grapes fresh, and perfect hill slopes for good drainage and thus flavourful wines. The most overrated region is Montepulciano, where high yields and sandy soils can make for flabby reds: look only for the top farmers here, not the bigger names who live off their reputation.

With a few honourable exceptions, Tuscan producers are still feeling their way with Burgundy's Pinot Noir, which finds Tuscany a bit too hot, and Syrah, which has worked well both on its own (at Isole e Olena, for example) and blended with Sangiovese. Plantings of other late-ripening grapes like Bordeaux's Petit Verdot and the southern French Mourvèdre (Spain's Mataro) appear to show promise.

Other emerging areas include Montecucco in Grosseto province and the Orcia Valley between Montalcino and Montepulciano, for reds rather than whites.

The "reds rather than whites" theme in Tuscany is a common one. Tuscans have always been a bit touchy about their lack of world class dry white wines. However, Vermentinos and, to a lesser extent, Chardonnay whites from the Etruscan coast down into Grosseto province (which also boasts Ansonica) show lovely softness of fruit with mouth-watering cores, with Vermentino (a native of neighbouring Liguria) especially impressive, and certainly Tuscany's most underrated white wine grape. You could also make a case for Ansonica on the Costa Argentario, but too little is produced for definitive judgments.

BELOW *A mural at one of Tuscany's pioneering organic wineries (see p.64).*

The white wines

Although it's too hot on the coast for aromatic whites like Sauvignon Blanc, they do thrive further inland, the Pinot Bianco (Pinot Blanc) performs brilliantly (with Chardonnay) in Querciabella's "Batàr" from Chianti Classico. Cooler, hillier inland sites around Pitigliano in Grosseto, and around Carmignano, Pomino, and Colline Lucchesi, plus the odd find further north around Colli dei Luni show that Tuscany can produce superb dry white wine, but most producers do seem to focus their attentions on reds. Generally, though, Tuscan whites show easy flavours of tropical fruit rather than more complex mineral-like ones.

And there is always Vernaccia di San Gimignano, which deserves to be more than just a picnic quaffer for day-trippers to "Tuscany's Manhattan", although the allowing of Chardonnay in the blend is seen by many as a backward step for the region, while accepting that it is a good short-term measure for generating sales. And Vernaccia can make some of Tuscany's best sparkling wines.

ABOVE *Sadly not all Tuscan road signs are as bright, or easy to read, as this.*

Historically, white Tuscan grapes, like the usually dull Trebbiano, the potentially exciting and creamy Malvasia, and the lime-twist-flavoured Grechetto, were blended into Chianti reds to give the wines some freshness (necessary in the days before temperature control during winemaking).

Now the laws have been changed, these white grapes are either being dumped into dreary whites labelled *Galestro*, after a common Tuscan soil type, or they are being grubbed up in favour of Merlot and Cabernet, or being used for *vin santo*. This intense white from late-picked, dried grapes ages in nearly filled barrels for several years and is sipped reverently at the end of a meal (a *vino da meditazione* or "meditation wine"). Drier examples go well with dessert, but try sweeter ones with dried fruit or cheese. *Vin santos* with a proportion of red grapes are labelled *Occhio di Pernice*, or "partridge-eye", after their colour.

The best Tuscan *vin santos* rank with Italy's greatest "dessert" wines, such is their power and complex range of flavours. Some, like Avignonesi's Occhio di Pernice, are far too hyped and expensive for what they are, so you'd be better off looking for *passito* red wines made along the Etruscan coast and on Elba from the Aleatico grape. These are dried on mats to concentrate them before pressing and fermentation, and provide moreish, simple pleasure, with generous sweetness.

Food and wine culture

I f you compliment Tuscans on their food, expect them to say somewhat over-modestly that "ours is only poor peasant food", the so-called *cucina povera*. This is a legacy of Tuscany's historic rural peasant tradition, the near-feudal *mezzadria* system whereby sharecrop farmers would give all but a small part of each year's harvest to the local landowner.

Living off the land

Hence Tuscans have learned to make do with whatever seasonal ingredients are freely available, be they truffles, wild chestnuts and mushrooms, game, the ubiquitous and spicy olive oil, or locally produced beef and cheese, plus of course seafood.

Antipasti

Common Tuscan appetizers include toast topped with chicken liver (*crostini di fegatini*) or toast covered in olive oil, diced tomatoes, and basil (*bruschetta*).

When eating *al fresco* try *fettunta*, prepared by rubbing garlic then drizzling olive oil on Tuscan bread (*pane toscano*), which, because it is unsalted, does not mask the oil's flavour. Take a bottle of sparkling (*spumante* or *frizzante*) wine with you.

Cold cuts like salt-cured ham (*prosciutto*) or air-dried, uncooked sausages (*salame*) are great with Tuscan rosé (*rosato toscano*) or freshly fermented reds drawn straight from the vat (*vino novello*). Try Florence's *salame finocchiona*, a sausage with fennel seeds, with Chianti Colli Fiorentini.

Primi piatti

The first course is invariably soup, made from vegetables, chickpeas (*ceci*) or beans (*fagioli*). Day-old bread soups flavoured with tomato, garlic, and basil (*pappa al pomodoro*) or with beans and dark green cabbage (*ribollita*) use up the leftovers and are supremely filling Tuscan classics. Try with moderate to firm reds like Carmignano or a decent Chianti Classico.

Thick, hand-rolled spaghetti called *pinci* in Montalcino or *pici* in Siena is often served with game sauce (*con ragout*), or with breadcrumbs fried in garlic and olive oil (*briciole di pane soffritte nell'olio*). Pasta dishes are eaten with a fork (spoons are considered bad manners). Try with Chianti Colli Senesi, Rosso di Montalcino or Chianti Colline Pisane.

RIGHT *Tuscany's colourful markets are full of local seasonal produce.*

BELOW *Many farmers advertise their wares on the side of the road.*

Secondi piatti

Fish from the Etruscan coast or freshwater fish cooked on reeds (*brustico*) suits Vernaccia di San Gimignano or Pomino Bianco. While Livorno's famous fish stew (*cacciucco*) stands up well to the richer, oak fermented Maremma dry white wines and is said to contain one type of fish for each letter "c" in its name.

Reds from Pomino, Montecucco, Bolgheri, and Chianti Rufina should aid digestion when tackling locally hunted wild boar (*cinghiale*), hare (*lepre*), rabbit (*coniglio*), and other game.

In Florence carnivores will be tempted by the huge "*La Fiorentina*" T-bone steaks. The meat comes from the unusually long-legged Chianina cattle and is served rare. Try with serious reds from Bolgheri. Juicier coastal reds like Morellino di Scansano suit roast suckling pig (*porchetta*), while crisp reds from Colli Aretini offset the thick texture of beef stewed in whatever local red is available (*stracotto*).

As well as vegetables, side dishes (*contorni*) include Mount Amiata chestnuts (*le castagne dell'Amiata*) and mushrooms.

Formaggi

Tuscany's most famous cheese is made from unpasteurized ewes' milk (*pecorino*) in the Val d'Orcia. Eat it in spring with uncooked broad beans (*baccelli*). Milder *marzolino* is produced in March, when the cows graze the spring grass. The ricotta-like *ravaggiolo* is drained on reeds and when made from goats' milk is delicious with local honey. Try soft red wines like Morellino di Scansano, or offset the savouriness with sweeter whites like Moscadello di Montalcino, or Aleatico *passito* from Elba.

DOLCI AND LA PASTICCERIA

Tuscan desserts are notably uncomplicated. Cakes are popular and **fruit cakes (*torte*)** can be lightly soaked in *vin santo* for extra moisture, though they are rarely heavy.

The exception is Siena's **panforte cake of candied fruit and nuts,** or **panpepato** which has spices such as cinnamon added; both go with Moscadello di Montalcino, or a glass of grappa.

Twice-baked biscuits (*biscotti*) include *ricciarelli*, made from marzipan, or the **cantucci** of Prato which contain almonds. They are often dunked in a glass of *vin santo*. **"Dead men's bones" (*ossi di morto*)** biscuits from Montalcino are softened with coffee instead.

The cream cheese and coffee confection ***tiramisù* or "pick me up"** is a Tuscan invention but a hard match for wine.

How to get there

A s a tourist magnet, Tuscany is well served by various transport links. However, Tuscany's size and topography mean that you will save both time and money if you know which particular bit of the region you are aiming for.

By air
Tuscany's two main airports are Florence's Amerigo Vespucci (tel: 055 3061300; www.aeroporto.firenze.it; code FLR) and Pisa's Galileo Galilei (tel: 050 849111; www.pisa-airport.com; code PSA). Both accept international flights.

Both Pisa and Florence airports are located some way from the town centres, but there is a range of transport options. Taxis are easily available at either airport, but you must have cash (euros) rather than plastic to pay your fare.

A mainline train service links Pisa airport to Florence's Santa Maria Novella train station. Remember to validate your ticket before you board a train, using the yellow machine on the platforms. As a cheaper option, bus services operate from both airports. You must buy tickets in the airport building before boarding buses, and, as with the trains, you must validate your ticket immediately whenever you board a bus, to avoid being fined.

For intercontinental flights, Rome's Fiumicino airport (tel: 06 65951; www.adr.it; code FCO) is closer to Tuscany than Milan's Linate (tel: 02 74852200; www.sea-aeroportimilano.it; code LIN/LIML).

Budget flights
No-frills airlines in Europe offer cheap flight deals to Genoa's Cristoforo Colombo airport (tel: 010 6015410; www.airport.genova.it; code GOA) in Liguria, which is useful for anyone visiting Lucca and the north Tuscan coast. Or instead try Perugia's Aeroporto Sant'Egidio (tel: 075 592141; www.airport.umbria.it; code PEG) in Umbria, which is handy for Arezzo in eastern Tuscany.

However, if you decide to fly to Ancona's Falconara (tel: 071 28271; www.ancona-airport.com; code AOI/LIPY) in the Marches you'll face a three-hour drive across the Apennines to get to Tuscany, and that's if there's no snow.

You can also fly to Emilia-Romagna, but to get from there to Florence the slow (toll-free) S67 road from Forlì's Aeroporto Forlimpopoli (tel: 0543 780049; code FRL/LIPK) will test your patience more than the quicker (tolls apply) A1 autostrada

BELOW *Useful maps and information can be found on the roadside.*

from Bologna's G Marconi airport (tel: 051 6479615; www.bologna-airport.it; code BLQ/LIPE).

By road

Florence is 267km (169 miles) from Rome, 296km (185 miles) from Milan, 1,410km (880 miles) from Calais, and 1,700km (1,062 miles) from Madrid. Mountain passes through the Alps often close in winter due to snow.

Italian motorways (*autostrade*) are much quicker and safer than national roads (*Strade Statali* or *SS*) or provincial roads (*Strade Provinciali* or *SP*) but are subject to tolls.

Tuscany is hard on cars: main roads are poorly surfaced and backwoods roads are generally unsurfaced. You'll need snow chains in winter. Buy them in advance, as many garages suddenly close when the snow comes.

The Automobile Club Italiano (ACI) is based in Rome (Via Marsala, 8, 00185 Roma; tel: 06 49981) but has offices throughout Italy and can recommend help in an emergency.

Coach travellers should contact Eurolines (www.eurolines.com) for international coach services running across Europe to Florence and Pisa.

ABOVE *Drainage canals transformed the marshy Maremma into prime vineyard land on the Etruscan coast.*

By train

Train travel within Italy is good value, despite supplements being payable on the fast Eurostar and Intercity trains. Those aged under 26 receive reductions. For booking information contact Italian Railways (from Italy only tel: 89 20 21; or visit the website www.trenitalia.com).

For information on train and motorail (if you are planning to take your own car) travel from continental Europe you can contact German Railways (www.bahn.de), Rail Europe (www.railsavers.com), France's Société Nationale des Chemins de Fer (SNCF) (www.voyages-sncf.com or www.sncf.com) or Eurostar (www.eurostar.co.uk), whose service connects from Paris to Florence via overnight sleeper.

Book way ahead as trains get overbooked in summer.

Where to stay

The wealth of accommodation options available for potential visitors to Tuscany is breathtaking, ranging from villas, apartments, farmhouses, castles, palaces, and former monasteries to the usual selection of bed and breakfasts, hotels (*alberghi*), local inns and guesthouses (*locande*), and rooms for the night in private houses (*affittacamere*). Remember that the star system of grading establishments offering accommodation in Italy reflects the kind of facilities on offer (*en suite*, internet) rather than furnishings, decorations, or service.

RIGHT *National pride flies high.*

BELOW Agriturismi *are a good way of seeing "real" Tuscany.*

Bed and breakfast

If you go for the bed and breakfast option, make sure you know what kind of breakfast you'll get: either continental, which means fruit juice, coffee, and a pastry, or something more substantial. Most bed and breakfast recommendations in this book are described as "average" in terms of price (from 40 to 70 euros), based on two people sharing, with breakfast. Many only accept cash. *See* the Italian bed and breakfast website for more information: www.bbitalia.it.

Self-catering holiday homes

Larger groups or families should consider renting a holiday home or an apartment on a farm or vineyard, called an *agriturismo* (agritourism). These are plentiful on wine estates and other farms which have converted outbuildings (*case coloniche*) once used by subsistence farmers, using restoration grants provided by the European Union. The best ones are booked out up to one year in advance by Dutch, Swiss, German, and American visitors, so be prepared to think well ahead.

Location is key, and is the biggest influence on price. What you need to consider is whether you just want a simple base, with washing machine for example, or if you want to play host during your stay and have big family meals.

If the latter, you need to find out how far away the nearest shops and markets, are and when they are open. Some of the more isolated villages may have produce suppliers delivering essentials like bread, for example, two or three times a week, in the absence of shops.

Often, the estate will offer home cooking on a pay as you eat basis in what they will call a *ristorante* but what is in fact a glorified home kitchen. Take advantage, as this can be some of the most authentic and best value cooking in Tuscany, as the money you spend goes on food rather than fancy tablecloths and stemware.

Do check whether yours is the only *agriturismo* on larger properties and, if so, if facilities like gardens, swimming pools, children's play areas, and garages are shared. Also check whether rentals run for a weekend or a whole week, whether you must pay utility bills, or for any firewood you use for heating or barbecues, and whether the bed linen is covered by the rental agreement.

Also, check whether your possessions are covered by the lessee's house insurance policy in case of theft, and what your cancellation rights are regarding deposits if you find you have to cancel. Finally, make sure who is responsible for cleaning the accommodation after you leave. Many *agriturismi* will only allow (often expensive) contract cleaners to do the job, so read the small print first.

Camping and caravanning

Camping can offer great value, especially if you book at least six months ahead for July and August, and then you get lucky with the weather. However, do check how the fees are calculated, either per person or per vehicle, and also how far you'll be from local towns. Bring mosquito repellent if you plan to camp in the Maremma.

Campsites are rated on a one- to four-star system, with four-star sites offering the most in terms of facilities. Pitching tents on private land is unwise, not just because you can be prosecuted, but you may also end up getting shot, by accident, by hunters who have free rein over large parts of the countryside, including private land.

The Federazione Italiana del Campeggio e del Caravanning (Via Vittorio Emanuele, 11, 50041 Calenzano (FI); tel: 055 882391; www.federcampeggio.it) has a list of campsites in Tuscany and a useful map. Touring Club Italiano also publishes a listing of campsites, the *Campeggi e Villaggi Turistici* (*see* www.campeggiitalia.com).

THE BEST GUIDEBOOKS

. . . .

The Italian Wine Guide by the Touring Club Italiano. **English. Follows the official wine routes. Also lists the winemaking rules for each region – making it a very dry read.**

Mangia e bevi in Toscana by Vanni Bolognesi, Alfredo Palmieri, and Daniel Thomases; published by Loggia de' Lanzi. **Breaks Tuscany down into regions and recommends restaurants, wineries, wine shops, and olive oil producers. Italian only.** www.loggiadelanzi.it

Osterie d'Italia, published by Slow Food. **Annual guide to eateries on a** comune **by** comune **basis, which makes it easy to find somewhere to eat if you know where you are.**

ABOVE *Many of Tuscany's famous reds are aged in oak.*

Youth hostels

Tuscan youth hostels are run by the Associazione Italiana Alberghi per la Gioventù. To stay in one you need to have joined the worldwide Youth Hostel Association (membership renewable annually), but you can do this when you arrive at your first Italian youth hostel. Youth hostels in places like Florence and Siena are hard to get into in summer without a prior booking.

Hotels and guesthouses

The hotel rating system in Italy is similar to that for campsites – a one-to-four star system based on the types of facilities offered and not on overall quality: the size of bedrooms, room service, phone and internet access, and so on. If travelling by car, check that your hotel has parking and, if so, that you won't have to enter a controlled zone for residents only to get there – otherwise your car number-plate may be photographed by cameras (in Siena, for example) and you might incur a hefty fine.

Monasteries and convents

Contact local tourist offices if you fancy a more ascetic stay in Tuscany in one of the region's many convents or monasteries. Rooms are usually single-sex and spartan, but they will be clean. You'll need to book ahead. Late nights are out, as curfews usually apply.

Working organic weekends

If you are looking to stay in Tuscany and get as close to the people as possible, why not contact World-Wide Opportunities on Organic Farms (WWOOF). In return for food, accommodation, and maybe some pocket money, you help out on the farm or vineyard for a weekend, a week, or even longer. *See* www.wwoof.org for how to become a member, or *see* www.wwoof.it for contact details of the scheme's coordinator in Tuscany.

The winemakers

The question "Who makes Tuscan wine?" is one answered only with some difficulty, such has been the pace of change in this iconic Italian wine region over the last 30 years. Thirty years ago Tuscan wines were made either on a small scale by the vineyard owners themselves, who would sell from the farm gate to local restaurants and grocery shops, or by the larger merchants and wine cooperatives whose huge economies of scale meant they could pile wine high and sell it cheap via the emerging retail chains and supermarkets.

Maintaining traditional roles

Both ends of this spectrum remain largely unchanged, except that Tuscan merchants like Antinori, Frescobaldi, Cecchi, and Ruffino have become more powerful, and their success has tempted them to buy up vineyards all over Italy. Likewise merchants from other parts of Italy, like Zonin and Gruppo Italiano Vini (GIV), have bought wineries in Tuscany (Zonin in San Gimignano with Casale and GIV with the merchant Melini).

Trading on the name

Despite producing some of Tuscany's most expensive wines, some of these merchants still manage to produce awful wine, especially at the cheaper end, for this is wine produced for supermarkets, who effectively now control how the bulk of our wine is produced. Sales are encouraged by slick marketing campaigns which rely on glossy photos containing blue Tuscan skies, pristine lines of cypress trees, and weed-free vineyards. But many of these mass-produced wines are anything but pristine. Antinori's marketing, for example, says the family has been making wine for 700 years; but some of the company's cheaper reds, such as "Santa Cristina" certainly don't reflect this heritage.

Thankfully what has changed over the last 30 years is the emergence of Tuscan producers who, although a respectable size, are too minnow-like to be granted a meeting with the supermarket supremos. One thinks of: Fontodi, Isole e Olena, and Riecine in Chianti Classico; Selvapiana in Chianti Rufina; Salicutti and La Torre in Montalcino; Terra d'Arcoiris in Colli Senesi; Casale (Falchini) and Montenidoli in San Gimignano; Valgiano in Colline Lucchesi; Mantellasi and Massavecchia in Grosseto amongst many. All are run in a hands-on fashion, as you'll see when you shake the owners' wine-soaked hands if you meet them during the winemaking period.

BELOW *A piece of history retained for posterity.*

Balancing the books

Larger Tuscan wineries have proved an attractive option for many financial institutions. Italian law states that insurance companies and banks must invest a percentage of their profits in agricultural activity, with tax benefits in return. However, winemakers find it harder to take creative risks when working for banks or insurance companies, invariably having to justify their profit and loss every financial quarter to shareholders.

Many critics feel Tuscan wines are becoming standardized because of too much interference from external consultants who are something of a safety net for winery owners nervous at having to compete in an increasingly cut-throat market. Of course, the consultants argue, Tuscans are too stubborn to follow their instructions to the letter, so how can the wines be standardized? But I think you can pick up stylistic similarities in Tuscan red wines from different wineries where consultants such as Alberto Antonini (crispness), Carlo Ferrini (chocolatey flavours), Stefano Chioccioli and Lorenzo Landi (black, rather than red in colour, fruit a dominant character), Franco Bernabei (linear elegance), or Attilio Pagli and Luca D'Attoma (bright rather than textured fruit) have been involved.

In the vineyard, too, consultants are playing a key part, and increasingly they are offering organic and Biodynamic counsel, the climate and mentality being predisposed to non-chemical solutions. These organic consultants come from abroad, such as Australia's Alex Podolinsky and France's François Bouchet for Biodynamics and Uwe Hofmann from Germany for organics.

BELOW *Vines and forest stretch as far as the eye can see.*

How Tuscany makes wine

There is so much poetry and flowery language surrounding the appreciation of wine that to talk about it in a more technical sense can come as something of a shock. Nevertheless, wine is simply Mother Nature's mid-point between grape juice and vinegar. It is made when sugars in grape juice are turned into alcohol by the action of yeast in a process we call fermentation; but leave a bottle of wine unstoppered and bacteria will quickly sour it and turn it into vinegar.

Going wild
There is a trend, in Tuscany and elsewhere, towards allowing naturally occurring wild yeasts to start the fermentation. These yeasts, found on the skins of the grapes and in the winery atmosphere, can give more complex flavours than commercially prepared yeasts, which do tend to make each tank of wine taste almost exactly the same as its neighbour. The winemaker sacrifices some control over the process in the hope of gaining complexity.

After the yeasts have fermented the sugar to alcohol, they die and sink to the bottom, forming a sludge called lees. If the grapes were healthy at harvest time, the wine can be left on the lees for a few days, weeks, or even months. This will make the wine's flavours extra-rich.

However, if the grapes are unhealthy, the lees will make the wine smell dirty, and the wine must be drawn off (racked) into clean tanks as quickly as possible.

ABOVE *Work in the vineyard is a year-round occupation.*

Dry white wine
The grapes are pressed and the juice collected in tanks, small oak barrels, or large wooden ovals for fermentation. Pips and skins are discarded. White fermentations usually last from several days to a couple of weeks. The temperature is normally controlled to 14–20°C (57–68°F). Any hotter, and the wines would lose their delicacy.

Basic dry Tuscan white is best drunk within a maximum couple of years of the harvest. To keep it as fresh as possible, it is bottled within six months. More expensive versions, such as the best Vernaccias from San Gimignano, or top whites like Querciabella's Batàr, wholly or partly fermented in oak barrels, are bottled within 18 months of the harvest. They will go on

improving in bottle for several years, and can age for a decade or more.

Most white winemakers in Tuscany prefer not to allow a spontaneous secondary fermentation, called the malolactic, to occur. This turns appley-tasting malic acid into buttery-tasting lactic acid, but as Tuscany is a hot region most white wines are usually soft enough without encouraging the malolactic.

Sparkling wines

There are two types of sparkling wine or *spumante* made in Tuscany. The first and most expensive is labelled *metodo classico* and is made in the same way as Champagne. A dry white wine is made in the normal way (the clear juice of red grapes can be used), and then bottled with a little yeast and sugar. This mixture creates a secondary fermentation in the sealed bottle. As the carbon dioxide created by the yeast cannot escape, it stays in the wine under pressure. The lees are allowed to settle in the neck of the bottle by turning it gradually upside-down over a period of weeks. The bottle neck is then frozen and the plug of ice and lees removed. The bottle is immediately topped up with more wine and corked for sale.

ABOVE *Large wooden vats updated with modern stainless-steel accessories.*

For cheaper sparkling wines the secondary alcoholic fermentation takes place in a sealed tank and the wine is then bottled under pressure. Such wines are labelled *metodo Charmat*, after the inventor of this process.

Vin santo and sweet white wines

Vin santo or "holy wine" is Tuscany's most famous dessert wine. The grapes are picked and then dried indoors for several months to shrivel them into raisins. This process, called the *appassimento*, concentrates the sugars through loss of water, so that when the grapes are pressed the juice is very thick. It is run into small barrels called *caratelli*, where it gradually ferments for at least three years. The bung is sealed with wax. If the barrels are filled right up, the wine tastes pure and sweet; if a larger head-space is left, the wine will be drier and more nutty-tasting. Sweet red wines made from dried red grapes, such as Aleatico on Elba, are called *passito* wines. Sweet white wines made from overripe, late-picked grapes shrivelled on the vine by a fungus that "nobly rots" them to concentrate the sugars are rare in Tuscany, as the late autumn climate is generally too dry for the fungus to form. *Vin santos* and *passito* wines labelled *liquoroso* have had alcohol added as spirit and are generally of poor quality.

Red wines

Unlike white wines, for red wines everything goes into the fermentation tank – juice, skins, and pips. Grape juice is clear in colour: the colour of red wine comes from the skins. The juice is therefore fermented with the skins, and the alcohol acts as a solvent, leaching colour and tannins into the wine. Tannins help red wines to age.

After picking, the grapes are separated from the stems and then crushed. The mush of juice, pips, and skins is pumped into fermenting vats. Most Tuscan winemakers feel leaving the stems in the tanks would create unwanted vegetal flavours, especially with Sangiovese, a variety that is prone to taste "weedy".

For red wine to get its colour and tannin, the increasingly alcoholic juice must be in contact with the skins. So juice is pumped from the bottom of the tank over the skins at the top. This is called, not surprisingly, pumping over (*rimontaggio* in Italian), and it usually happens every morning and evening.

Colour extraction is encouraged by heat, so red wine tanks are allowed to ferment at 26–35°C (79–95°F). Fermentation is usually over within a week or two. Afterwards, the young wine is left in contact with the skins for several more days or weeks to ensure maximum flavour and colour are extracted. Some winemakers still use an old Tuscan practice called *governo*, whereby the juice of dried grapes is added half-way through fermentation, creating softer wines. Ageing reds in barrel accentuates the red colour, important for Sangiovese, whose colour can lack a bit of depth.

One increasingly modern trend, though, is to take out the pips during or near the end of fermentation, as the phenolics in the pips accentuate Sangiovese's already bitter flavours.

After tasting each tank daily, the winemaker will decide when the wine can be run off the skins into tanks or oak barrels. The skins are then pressed. This press wine can be blended into the main wine in small amounts for extra structure.

Ageing red wines in large wooden ovals softens the aggressive side of grapes like Sangiovese. Smaller barrels, which give the wines a stronger, vanilla-like flavour, are now common in most Tuscan cellars.

Pink wines

Pink wine is made in the same way as red, but because only a moderate amount of colour is needed, the wine is drawn off the grape skins after only a few hours of fermentation.

CATCHING THE COOPER

If you want to see barrels being made, one artisan barrel-maker offering a free tour is **Agostini Luciano Bottaio** (Italian only; call ahead) at 40, Piazza Cavour in 55055 Ponte All'ania (LU); tel: 0583 709357.

Other good coopers include: **Borghesi Fratelli Fabbrica Botti** in Poggibonsi (SI); tel: 0577 936507, **Roselli Leonetto Botti Barili Tini**, also in Poggibonsi (SI); tel: 0577 937105, and **Carmignani Filippo Fabbrica di Botti Legno** in Rufina (FI); tel: 055 8397015.

BELOW *Ugly but functional: the reality behind the romantic Tuscan dream.*

Visiting producers and winery etiquette

You'd be hard pressed to find a more visitor-friendly region than Tuscany, especially for wine tourism. It is the lifeblood of the local economy. But to make your visits successful, try to bear the following general points in mind.

Dressing for the occasion

Italians dress to impress, so it pays to be as smart as possible. Shorts and a T-shirt are fine in the heat of summer, as long as they don't look like you've been wearing them for weeks on end or have just fished them out, unironed, from the bottom of your knapsack or suitcase.

Although you won't be expected to turn up wearing a jacket and tie, men should wear a shirt, not T-shirt, at the most aristocratic estates, although unripped jeans are fine.

You may think that Italians expect a kiss on both cheeks when greeting or saying goodbye; a handshake will suffice unless you have established a real friendship.

Planning ahead

Despite the fact that Tuscan wineries are inundated with requests for visits, you will undoubtedly be welcomed with open arms. Return the courtesy with punctuality. Ensure you arrive bang on time – not five minutes early or five minutes late.

Tuscany is Italy's fifth biggest region (out of 20). Distances between Tuscan wineries appear deceptively small on the map – so plan well ahead when booking appointments.

When booking, tell your potential host which other estates you are visiting locally. They can tell you whether your timings are realistic – especially in areas where the roads are unsurfaced or particularly slow-going.

RIGHT *Signs for wineries are generally plentiful – just watch out for local drivers.*

BELOW *Most wineries will proudly declare their location.*

At the winery

Most visits take from 30 minutes to an hour. Whereas in California or Burgundy you might taste up to half a dozen wines, in Montalcino or Montepulciano you could be offered just one wine, the latest vintage of red for example, or two if there is a *riserva*. The hosts will usually decide the order of tasting: white before red, dry before sweet, etc.

Wineries with dedicated tasting rooms may charge you a small fee, refundable (usually) if you make a purchase. This covers the cost of cleaning wine glasses and so on. Italian police are very

strict on drinking and driving, so make sure you nominate a designated (sober) driver if you are drinking rather than spitting the wine.

If you are tasting from bottle in a tasting room, a spittoon will usually be provided for you to empty your glass or spit the wine. Don't be embarrassed about spitting, or about asking for a napkin with which to wipe your mouth if things get messy. Even professional wine tasters have been known to get it wrong and dribble sometimes. If you are tasting in the cellar or winery instead, it is quite normal to spit wine out on the floor, or the drainage gutter under the lines of tanks or barrels, unless a spittoon has been provided.

When tasting the most expensive wines from barrel, allow the host to tip the remains of your glass back into the barrel if need be. Rinsing your glass with a little wine first to get rid of any dusty smells, or those picked up from drying cloths, is perfectly acceptable. It shows your host that you are serious and you want to see the wine at its best. The Italian verb for wine rinsing like this is "avvinare".

Tasting components

When tasting in the winery, you will taste from tank or barrel. Since this will probably not be the final blend, ask the producer what you are tasting.

What you are given to taste can also depend on the time of year. During harvest you will be offered a taste of the grape juice drawn straight from the press – for white wines – or the grape crusher – for reds. It will look a bit murky but will taste deliciously sweet.

Don't be afraid of tasting fermenting wines. They'll be a bit fizzy – carbon dioxide is given off by the yeast – but the fruit flavours are usually incredibly pronounced.

In the weeks after the harvest you may be offered a taste of each grape variety as it sits in tank, which is a great way of learning the differences. This might be Vernaccia and Chardonnay in San Gimignano, or Sangiovese, Canaiolo, and Cabernet Sauvignon in Chianti, for example. Wines from the different varieties are usually blended together in spring, so only then will you be offered a taste of the new blends.

Ask for a price list and write tasting notes on it as you taste. This provides a useful souvenir of your visit and will help you work out your favourite styles of wine. It will also show your host you are a wine lover, not a time-wasting tourist.

And lastly, if you see a winery you like the look of but you haven't made an appointment, you stand absolutely zero chance of being welcomed between 12.30pm and 2.30pm, for lunch in Italy is a religion. So always book ahead to avoid any possibility of disappointment.

DAYS TO AVOID: ITALIAN PUBLIC HOLIDAYS (*FESTIVITA*)

JANUARY: 1 New Year, Nuovo Anno; **6** Epiphany, **Epifania**. **MARCH/APRIL:** Good Friday, **Venerdì Santo**; Easter Monday, **Pasquetta**. **APRIL: 25** National Holiday, **Festa della liberazione**. **MAY: 1** Labour Day, **Festa dei lavoratori**. **JUNE: 2** Republic or National Day, **Festa della Repubblica**. **AUGUST: 1–15** Italy shuts down for holidays*; **15** Feast of the Assumption of the Virgin Mary, **Ferragosto**. **NOVEMBER: 1** All Saints' Day, **Tutti i Santi**. **DECEMBER: 8** Immaculate Conception, **Immacolata Concezione**; **25** Christmas Day, **Natale**; **26** Boxing Day, **Santo Stefano**.

*August 1–15: estates offering *agriturismo* will stay open – just note the owners may not be around.

Time out from wine

I t is easier than you think to escape from wine while in Tuscany. You can of course spend your time as a "culture vulture", exploring Tuscany's thousands of churches, art galleries, and historic buildings; but there are also so many other things for tourists as well as locals to do, so try some of these.

Top sporting action

Football is an Italian obsession, and Tuscany has three teams in Italy's top division called *Serie A*: Siena (www.acsiena.it), Livorno (www.livornocalcio.it), and the unpredictable (and recently bankrupted) Fiorentina (www.fiorentina.it). You can buy tickets to most matches on the day, or in advance from the clubs or local ticket offices (the local bus station in Siena's case, for example). Rugby is becoming more popular in Italy, with Florence the leading local team (*see* www.firenzerugby.it), while Siena's basketball team, Siena Mens Sana, has the town's strongest fan base (www.menssanabasket.it).

Italians love cycling, too, and the Giro d'Italia (second only to the Tour de France) passes through Tuscany in May. If you want to get on a bike yourself, contact Gli Amici della Bicicletta at Via Campansi, 32 in Siena (tel: 0577 45159; www.comune.siena.it/adb). It provides details of local bike hire and the best cycling routes in towns and across country.

Ski lovers should head to Tuscany's main resort at Abetone, in the Apennine mountains. It offers cross-country and piste skiing, plus ice-skating and snowboarding from December to March. For information on ski hire, ski passes, and snow bulletins contact Abetone's Agenzia per il Turismo Informazioni Accoglienza Turistica (tel: 0573 60231; www.abetone.com).

Tuscany's coast and islands offer many opportunities for watersports fans. Fish for sea bass and bream from ports like Castiglione della Pescaia, Follonica, and Marina di Grosseto on the southern Tuscan coast.

If you want freshwater fishing for salmon, eel, and catfish on a man-made lake, try Azienda Agricola Venere in Foiano Della Chiana in Arezzo province (tel: 0575 640399; www.paginegialle.it/lagovenere), or Azienda Agricola Soiano in Montaione in Florence province (tel: 0571 698223; www.paginegialle.it/soiano). Both offer accommodation. You will need a permit from the Federazione Italiana Pesca Sportiva Sezione Provinciale in Firenze (tel: 055 354768).

For watersports fans the Monte Argentario promontory, and especially the island of Elba, in Grosseto province is full of

RIGHT *Amiatino donkeys are named after Mount Amiata in Grosseto province.*

BELOW *Wild boar is a Tuscan specialty, usually for gastronomes rather than modern artists.*

places to snorkel and scuba-dive. On Elba contact Portoferraio's tourist office (tel: 0565 914671) for accredited diving schools. The best waves for windsurfing are found in the Costa Fiorita (see box, below).

Regional parks cover the Apuane alps (www.parcapuane.it), where you can go trekking on the "trail of the wolf" in the Garfagnana; the area west of Pisa around Magliarino, San Rossore, and Massaciuccoli (www.parks.it/parco. migliarino.san.rossore), and the Maremma (www.parco-maremma.it). Contact the Butteri d'Alta Maremma Associazione if you want to herd cattle and wild horses with the local cowboys (tel: 0588 37865; www.butteri-altamaremma.com).

Cooking Tuscan style

Or you can learn how to cook at one of Tuscany's many cookery schools. Many wineries can organize cookery course days if you plan ahead, and it's always cheaper for groups. For something more structured try cookery schools at Chianti Classico wineries like Vicchiomaggio and Badia a Coltibuono (see pp.44 and 54) or contact Turin's Instituto Culinario Italiano per Stranieri (Italian Cookery Institute for Foreigners) at Corso Re Umberto, 30, 10128 Torino (tel: 11 549595) to find out what's on offer.

Pampering and performing

If you feel you need to de-stress and detox, visit spas or terme at Casciana Terme (see Pisa chapter, p.70), Saturnia (see Grosseto chapter, p.132), Chianciano Terme (see Siena chapter, p.74), Petriolo (Grosseto province), or the incredibly clean Calidario in Venturina (Livorno province).

And at the end of a long day, get your culture fix by attending an open-air classical music concert performed by the Accademia delle Crete Senesi (for details email: info@orchestredeschampselysees.com). These are held every August in Pienza, Monticchiello, Monte Oliveto (famous for the monastery built by San Benedetto), and the monastery at Sant'Anna in Camprena where the Oscar-winning film, The English Patient, was partly shot. For concerts later in the year (classical or jazz), plus news of theatre productions see Florence's website (www.firenze.net) for the latest news.

OTHER ACTIVITIES AVAILABLE IN TUSCANY

Windsurfing: Contact the Costa Fiorita Booking Centre (tel: 0586 759059; info@costafiorita.it).

Walking: Tuscany has two national parks, the marine park (www.islepark.it) which includes volcanic islands like Elba and Montecristo (as in The Count of Montecristo), and the Parco Nazionale delle Foreste Casentinesi Monte Falterona Campiglia (www.parks.it/parco. nazionale.for.casentinesi/).

How to get your wine home

The most elite Tuscan estates don't sell direct to the public. Instead you'll have to be content with a ration of sometimes just two bottles per person of the top wines from local wine stores or *enoteche*.

RIGHT *The straight, tree-lined roads take you through the beautiful countryside.*

BELOW *There are rather more sophisticated ways of transporting your wine home.*

Buying in bulk

However, from less elite estates it is easy to buy wine in bulk (*vino sfuso*) direct from the tank or barrel, by the demi-john (*in damigiana*) which you can bring yourself or buy at the winery, usually from 10 to 54 litres (and usually glass rather than plastic), in bottle (*a bottiglia*) or by the 12- or 6-bottle case (*a casse* or *a cartone*).

The tax question

Italian law obliges you to collect a receipt (*scontrino*) when purchasing anything from wine shops or vineyards. Non-EU residents may claim a refund on Italy's sales tax (*Imposta sul Valore Aggiunto* or *IVA*) of around 20% on wine and 4% on olive oil, for example. You must spend more than 155 euros in total, and make sure that the receipt you obtain describes the goods in detail (*i.e.* includes the wine name, bottle sizes, quantity) and shows you as the buyer.

For this reason you will need to carry your passport when making purchases – not easy if this is also required by your hotel. Present the paperwork at the Customs Office at the airport or border when you leave Italy. Tax refunds are much easier if you buy in "Euro Tax Free" shops – but wineries are not usually registered as such.

Bringing wine home

You don't need to be a genius to work out that wine is fragile, heavy, and unwieldy. I have lost count of the number of times I have seen suitcases sodden by red wines that have got crushed in transit. And airlines are getting increasingly strict about the weight allowances for carry-on luggage so check before you buy too much.

The baggage allowance of the cross-channel train service Eurostar (tel: 08705 186186) is two large items and one small item per person. If you can tape a couple of smaller wine boxes together, this will count as one item.

Post-haste
Posting your wine home is another option, if you can find the right way of packaging it – usually a polystyrene single-bottle tube set in a cardboard sheath. Some wineries may have these for sale – but don't bank on it. For international shipping try the Internet Train internet *caffè* in Siena (Via Pantaneto; 54, 53100 Siena; tel: 0577 247460, email: sienashipping@gmail.com), which is more helpful than the big courier firms, especially regarding shipments of fragile goods to North America.

Posting wine and olive oil home would make financial sense only if either are fairly to very expensive – but you would need to insure it as well as pay the high postage costs. You can't post wine to the USA, where each state has its own rules on the importation of alcohol, and the federal government has increasingly stringent restrictions on wine. It is classed as a food product, so its label must conform to the USA's byzantine, absurd, and protectionist labelling laws.

Fill your boots
Transporting wine within the European Union (EU) is fairly straightforward, as long as it is for personal consumption and not for resale once it has crossed a border.

Cross-channel "booze cruisers" have complained of persecution by the UK customs service, Her Majesty's Customs and Excise, so know your rights – and their rules. For advice on allowances, contact HM Customs and Excise National Advice Service (tel: 0845 010 9000; www.hmce.gov.uk).

The rules in brief
Any alcohol or tobacco you bring into the UK must be for your own use. You can take 90 litres of wine into the UK, which equates to 10 cases of 12 bottles (75cl). This is enough, the government says, for one person to drink up to half a litre of wine per day for six months!

If you wish to bring in more than this amount, expect to prove that either you are a very heavy drinker (via a doctor's note) or the wine is for a party or a wedding (provide invitations at the very least, or a signed letter from the vicar or registry office at best).

If Customs think that the goods are for a commercial purpose, they may seize them – as well as any vehicle used to transport them – and they may not return them to you.

If you are caught smuggling or selling alcohol, this may be seized, and for a serious offence you could be punished with up to seven years in prison.

Discovering
Vineyards in
Tuscany

Chianti Classico

W hen you think of Italian red wine you generally think Chianti; and when you think of Chianti, you cannot help but think that Chianti is the epitome of Tuscany: hills rolling like a carnival ride, the passengers emerald green cypress trees punching the sky, with skin-coloured terracotta roof tiles on stone farm buildings sunbathing under the blue, and vineyards as far as the eye can see.

Finding the best Chianti

The Chianti production zone lies between Florence and Siena, with Chiantis from all or part of the best nine villages of Barberino Val d'Elsa, Castellina in Chianti, Castelnuovo Berardenga, Gaiole in Chianti, Greve in Chianti, Poggibonsi, Radda in Chianti, San Casciano Val di Pesa, and Tavarnelle Val di Pesa allowed the Chianti Classico designation. Their wines carry the symbol of the black rooster or *il gallo nero* – see p.57 for the reason why.

Tourist trap

This is arguably Italy's most popular destination for tourists in general and wine tourists in particular: Dutch and German camper-vans clog the roads in high season – the Swiss come in family saloons – while the British presence is most associated with the ex-pats who renovated farmhouses in such numbers from the 1980s that the region acquired its most enduring Anglo-Saxon nickname of "Chiantishire".

The Siena–Florence hinterland today often resembles a battleground for parking spots and agritourism accommodation, but in medieval times it was a battleground of a different sort, as these two town republics fought for regional supremacy. The legacy of this conflict is fortified medieval towns (or *borgos*) like Mercatale, Tavarnelle, and San Casciano in the Pesa Valley (*Val di Pesa*) on the Chianti zone's western flank, and Greve, Gaiole, and Radda in the Greve Valley on its eastern flank.

Revised introspection

Not surprisingly for a people who were often holed up behind fortifications, Chianti's inhabitants are accused of being inward looking. True, they failed to adapt quickly enough when the straw-covered bottles (*fiaschi*) and the plonk-like wine style that went with them lost their appeal from the 1970s; but they have fought back, improving vineyard and winery practices, eliminating rules forcing white wine grapes into red wine

BELOW *The old-fashioned straw covering for Chianti bottles.*

665

WHERE TO EAT

Gelateria Antica (E3)
Via Vittorio Veneto, 68/70
50022 Greve in Chianti (FI)
Tel: 328 6222699
Ice cream plus pastries and homemade cakes like *torta margherita* (soft sponge with icing sugar), *mimosa* (cream sponge), and *crostate* (cherry and plum jam or marmalade tarts).

Osteria Mangiandomangiando (E3)
Piazza Matteotti, 80
50022 Greve in Chianti (FI)
Tel: 055 8546372
Closed Monday. Gnocchi and ravioli with seasonal sauces such as zucchini or artichoke, spelt, white bean soup, and green tagliatelle with vegetable sauce.

Ristorante Il Cavaliere (E4)
Via di Gabbiano, 12
50020 Mercatale
Val di Pesa (FI)
Tel: 055 8218423
ilcavaliere@
ilcavalieredigabbiano.it
www.ilcavalieredigabbiano.it
Closed Monday and Tuesday. Start with vegetable salad with liver pâté or sheeps' cheese and artichoke flan, followed by penne pasta with saffron, artichokes, and rosemary or roast leg of rabbit. Finish off with pears poached in Chianti.

Trattoria Oltre Il Giardino (D3)
Piazza Gastone
Bucciarelli, 42
50020 Panzano
in Chianti (FI)
Tel: 055 852828
www.ristorante
oltreilgiardino.it
Waist-widening starters such as deep-fried polenta with *porcini* mushrooms, tortelli stuffed with potatoes, or zucchini and ricotta risotto.

blends, and Chianti and Chianti Classico wines now account for around 60% of Tuscan wine sales. The vast majority are reds based on Sangiovese, with either local grapes like Canaiolo (for spice), Colorino (for colour), Malvasia Nera and Ciliegiolo (both for fruit), or French grapes like Cabernet (black fruit), Merlot (red fruit), and Syrah (for spice) blended in.

In addition, you'll find that most of the locals you'll come into contact with during your trip speak at least some English. This will help you to shop around, for even though Chianti is a tourist hotspot you are spoilt for choice, especially in terms of accommodation. You may consider staying north of Florence or south of Siena, just outside the zone, commuting in for visits which will save you money, even though Italy's fuel prices are usually amongst the highest in Europe; but this will chew up time, Florence being especially slow to traverse (much slower than Siena for example). And, as Chianti's road signs are often criticized for their vagueness, try to get the *consorzio's* wine route map (see p.41) as soon as you arrive. It will save hours of frustrating dead-ends.

Getting there
The Chianti and Chianti Classico zones essentially lie between Siena and Florence, so see details provided on pp.63 and 74.

Travelling around
Route summaries There are two possible itineraries for the Chianti Classcio region .
Route One summary This route covers the northern portion of Chianti, beginning in Florence, then heading south via Greve in Chianti to beyond Panano in Chianti where you turn west to San Donato in Poggio, before heading back to Florence via San Casciano Val di Pesa, Mercatale in Val di Pesa, and finally Impruneta. Total distance approximately 60km (37 miles). Allow two to three days at least.
Route Two summary This route covers the southern portion of Chianti, beginning in Siena and going in a north–south zig-zag through the hamlets of Ponte a Bozzone, Vagliagli, San Giusto in Salcio, Lecchi in Chianti, Pianella, and Barca to reach the town of Castelnuovo Berardenga, then north via San Gusme in Chianti and Castagnoli to reach Gaiole in Chianti, then via Coltibuono westwards to Radda in Chianti and Castellina in Chianti, then south via Fonterùtoli and Quercegrossa to Siena. Total distance approximately 90km (54 miles). Allow three or four days at least.

Route One: Chianti north
From Florence head south and find the SS222 (Chiantigiana) towards Siena. Before Greve in Chianti stop at Castello

Legend

- Chianti Classico
- Siena (Chianti Colli Senesi)
- Florence (Chianti Colli Fiorentini) and Montespertoli
- Chianti Rufina and Pomino

Route One: Chianti north
Allow two to three days at least

Route Two: Chianti south
Allow three or four days

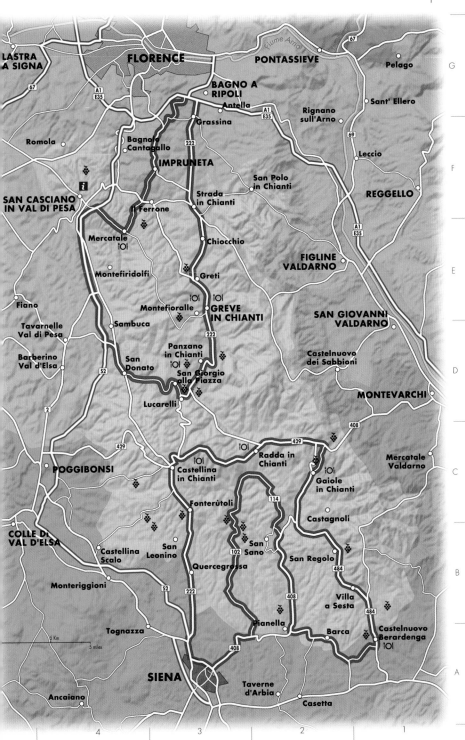

WINERIES IN CHIANTI NORTH

Castello dei Rampolla [D3]
Via Case Sparse, 22
50020 Panzano
in Chianti (FI)
Tel: 055 852001
castellodeirampolla.cast@tin.it

Castello Vicchiomaggio [D3]
Loc Le Bolle
Via Vicchiomaggio, 4
50022 Greve in Chianti (FI)
Tel: 055 854079
www.vicchiomaggio.it

Fattoria Casaloste [D3]
Via Montagliari, 32
50020 Panzano
in Chianti (FI)
Tel: 055 852725
www.casaloste.com

Fattoria Ispoli [F4]
Via Santa Lucia, 2
Fraz Mercatale Val di Pesa
50024 San Casciano
in Val di Pesa (FI)
Tel: 055 821613
www.fattoria-ispoli.com

Fattoria Poggiopiano [F3]
Via di Pisignano, 28/30
50026 San Casciano
in Val di Pesa (FI)
Tel: 055 8229629

Monte Bernardi [D3]
Via Chiantigiana, 68
50020 Panzano
in Chianti (SI)
Tel: 0577 852400
www.montebernardi.com

Tenuta Fontodi [D3]
Via San Leolino, 87
50020 Panzano
in Chianti (FI)
Tel: 055 852005
fontodi@fontodi.com
www.fontodi.com

Tenuta Vecchie Terre di Montefili [E3]
Via San Cresci, 45
50022 Greve in Chianti (FI)
Tel: 055 853739
www.vecchieterredimontefili.it

Vicchiomaggio (*see* box, left), which has been producing wine since at least 957AD. John and Paola Matta run a fairly priced cookery school here, with courses tailor-made for guests, allowing you to concentrate on fish, meat, or vegetarian dishes for example, or on mastering Tuscan specialties like *ribollita* soup or Florentine steaks. John Matta says the self-catering accommodation here "allows you to stay in a Renaissance castle for the price of Travelodge", with functional and unfussy rooms in an atmospheric setting. There is also a small hotel plus a wedding chapel, should you get carried away by the romance of Tuscany during your stay. The estate's smooth, fruity wines are available at its own shop-restaurant on the driveway leading to the castle.

In the centre of Greve take the road west towards the compact fortified medieval village of Montefioralle for Tenuta Vecchie Terre di Montefili (*see* box, left; by prior appointment). The Acuti family sold off their north-facing vineyards here, concentrating on warmer, south-facing sites in which later-ripening grapes like Cabernet would ripen fully. You can feel the ripeness in the "Bruno di Rocca" bottling, one of Tuscany's richer tasting Cabernet/Sangiovese reds. The "Anfiteatro" red, pure Sangiovese, shows wild fruit and is aged in large wooden ovals, which softens its firm tannins without making the wine too woody.

All is not wine

Near here there is a very good organic olive oil producer, Alfredo Gennari of the Podere Fede (tel: 055 960743), who has all the main varieties used in Tuscany, such as the Frantoio, which forms the backbone of most Tuscan olive oils, the Moraiolo, which is said to give the oil its peppery character, the Leccino, which gives breadth, and the Pendolino, which is planted mainly to pollinate the other trees. Gennari's trees are like many in Tuscany, relatively young trunks which were regrafted from the larger root systems after the terrible winter frosts of early 1985 killed the growth above ground of around 85% of Tuscan olive trees.

Dynamic wines from Querciabella

Other good wine producers around Greve include Paolina Savignola (tel: 055 8546036; savignola@ftbcc.it), whose small vineyard containing young but high quality cuttings of Sangiovese produces notably rich Chianti Classico and the Sangiovese-based red "Granaio"; and the Podere Poggio Scalette (tel: 055 8546108; poggio.scalette@tiscali.it), owned by one of Tuscany's leading winemaking consultants, Vittorio Fiore and his son, Yuri. The top wine here is the dense "Il Carbonaione" made from an old Sangiovese sub-variety,

planted in the 1930s, called Lamole. New cuttings of this
have been interplanted with the existing vines, in vineyards
just south of Greve overlooking the Querciabella estate
(www.querciabella.com). Here the well-drained and well-
exposed vineyards, Biodynamic wine-growing, low yields,
and careful winemaking have made this one of Tuscany's most
dynamic estates (visits are strictly by appointment only).

ABOVE *The terracotta roofs give
a warm feel to Tuscan towns.*

Owner Sebastiano Cossia Castiglioni produces the
cleverly blended "Camartina" from Sangiovese (for freshness),
Cabernet (for aroma), Merlot (for width), and Syrah (for
spice), as well as the intensely round dry white "Batàr" from
Chardonnay and 20-year-old Pinot Bianco vines. There are
separate red wine cellars here for the Bordeaux and Italian
grapes because Sangiovese is a much fussier grape in the
cellar than Cabernet Sauvignon. In the barrel-ageing cellars
the wines are mounted on rollers to make mixing the dead
yeast lees with the wines easier, with no need to pump. Yeast
lees can give wines more texture and prevent undue
oxidation. When it comes to racking the wine with pumps, an
ingenious system allows the contents of each barrel to go
back into the same one after the wine is racked off its lees.

Historic Vignamaggio

Close by is Vignamaggio (tel: 055 854661; www.
vignamaggio.com), whose cavernous wine cellars containing
seemingly every type of fermenting vessel and wine storage
tank lie under the wedding-cake-like pink villa in which
Mona Lisa (immortalized in Leonardo da Vinci's painting,
1503–6) is said to have been born and where the first
recorded use of the term Chianti is found in a letter of 1404.

Catching the sun

The vineyards around Panzano in Chianti enjoy a renowned
suntrap called the *conca d'oro*, or "golden bowl", perfectly
exposed to the southeast and famed for making unusually rich,

**WHERE TO EAT:
A USEFUL WEBSITE**

For menu updates, contact
details, and opening times
for the widest selection of
Chiantigiana restaurants,
see the website:
www.ristorantichianti.com

WHERE TO EAT

Enoteca Bengodi [A1]
Via Società Operaia, 11
53019 Castelnuovo
Berardenga (SI)
Tel: 0577 355116
enoteca.bengodi@libero.it
Closed Monday. Filling
but not too heavy *tagliatelle*
all'ortolana (*i.e.* with
seasonal vegetables).
Or try the stewed wild
boar or grilled meats.

**Ristorante Albergaccio
di Castellina [C3]**
Via Fiorentina, 63
53011 Castellina
in Chianti (SI)
Tel: 0577 741042
www.albergacciocast.com
Closed Sunday and
Wednesday lunch.
Mushroom and chestnut
soup, ravioli with wild
mushroom and duck liver,
lamb with aubergine,
pigeon with anchovies,
and black cabbage flan.
For serious foodies.

**Ristorante Giovanni
da Verrazzano [E3]**
Piazza Matteotti, 28
50022 Greve in Chianti (FI)
Tel: 055 853189
www.verrazzano.it
Closed Monday. Cookery
courses offered. Part
of a 10-room hotel.
Typical dishes include
roasted duck aromatized
with garlic and rosemary,
and Chianti Classico stew
(beef with carrots, onions,
and local wine).

La Tavolozza [C3]
Loc Croce Fiorentina, 32/34
53011 Castellina
in Chianti (SI)
Tel: 0577 741077
Good value family cooking,
with pork, mushroom, and
Chianti pasta, or steak
with *rucola* and cheese.

soft, ripe Chianti Classico that is drinkable relatively early – within about two years of the harvest, or not long after the wines have been released from their mandatory ageing period.

In fact, rather than there being a single bowl or "shell", there is a series of mini-amphitheatres, giving Sangiovese the sun it needs to get ripe. The vines are prevented from stressing in such hot conditions by the limestone in the sub-soil, which acts like a sponge, soaking up winter and spring rainfall, and releasing it slowly to the vines during summer and autumn.

Other recommended wineries

Wineries on the Greve side of Panzano, east of the town, include the following: Le Cinciole (www.lecinciole.it), whose Chianti Classico Riserva "Petresco" offers crowd-pleasingly soft fruit and oak; the Castellacci family's La Marcellina (tel: 055 852126; www.lamarcellinia.it), where the highest vines reach an above average 500 metres (1,640 feet) and where the top reds include "Comignole" and the Sangiovese/Cabernet Sauvignon "Camporosso" for its burst of young vine fruit; and the genial Andrea Sommaruga's Panzanello (www.panzanello.it; English spoken), which is also known as the Fattoria Sant'Andrea, offering value-for-money olive oil and organic Chianti Classico.

Organic altitude

The pick of the wineries in this area though is arguably Fattoria Casaloste (*see* p.44) which produces a mouth-watering range of Chianti Classicos from organic grapes, aged in French oak barrels for a plump, vanilla sheen. Small-berried clones of Sangiovese, plus a policy of low yields by owners Giovanni and Emilia Battista d'Orsi, make for wines with as much colour as flavour. Higher vineyards are being developed here, too, to provide as much zip as possible in the aftertaste.

Across the valley, west of Panzano on the Pesa Valley side, you'll find wineries like Fattoria La Massa (tel: 055 852722) which Giampaolo Motta bought in a run down state in the early 1990s, leaving the family tanning business in Naples to make wine. Motta worked at Riecine (*see* p.53) to learn the ropes, and made thick Chianti Classico reds, full of boisterous oak, but has since toned down the style, even in the "Giorgio Primo" bottling which mixes Merlot with Sangiovese. Other reliable performers here include Villa Cafaggio (tel: 055 852949), for clean, almost clinical Chianti Classicos and lightly honeyed *vin santo*, and Carlo Novarese's Carobbio (tel: 055 8560133; info@carobbiowine.com), where relatively low-lying vineyards produce warm-hearted Sangiovese reds like "Pietraforte" and "Leone del Carobbio".

Another much respected performer here is the de Napoli family's Castello dei Rampolla (*see* p.44), where oats and flowering clovers are sown amongst the vines to encourage beneficial insect predators, such as ladybirds and lacewings, and to stress the vines into lower yields by competing with the vine roots for water. This makes for chunky, thick red wines like the Chianti Classico and the usually consistent Chianti Classico Riserva, as well as the Cabernet Sauvignon-dominated "Sammarco" red. From the top of the tower you can get a fantastic view of Panzano's "golden bowl".

Food matching in the vineyard

South of Panzano you'll find Tenuta Fontodi (*see* p.44; by appointment), one of Tuscany's most respected and consistent performers over the last two decades for smooth Chianti Classico and Syrah, savoury Sangiovese reds like "Flaccianello", full-bodied dry whites, and thick *vin santo*. The striking gravity-fed winery contains spacious barrel halls and red wine vats in which the skins can be punched down into the fermenting wine automatically. In the vineyards, owner Giovanni Manetti keeps a herd of Chianina cows to provide manure for compost, fertilizing the soil. When mature, the cows are butchered at the renowned Macelleria Checcucci, one of Panzano's two butchers; the other is the flamboyant Dario Cecchini of the Antica Macelleria Cecchini (closed Monday). The Manetti family's 400-year-old terracotta business has even been called on by the Uffizi Gallery in Florence during its many restorations.

Continue south on the SS222 to Monte Bernardi (*see* p.44; by appointment), run by engaging and energetic siblings Michael and Jennifer Schmelzer. The tiny cellar is cut into the hillside, with bare rock exposed above the wine press and fermenting vats. Bright, unfiltered Chianti Classicos with a confident mineral edge, the firm 100% Sangiovese "Sa'etta",

LEFT *Take a stroll along a meandering track through the vineyards.*

BELOW *Refresh yourself at the municipal water fountains.*

WHERE TO EAT

Porta del Chianti
Piazza Castelli, 12
53010 San Gusme (SI)
Tel: 0577 358010
Small, inviting restaurant away from the usual Chianti crowds, offering tender lamb or beef with chickpea purée.

Taverna del Guerrino [E3]
Via Montefioralle, 39
50022 Greve in Chianti (SI)
Tel: 055 853106
Small restaurant with good seasonal greens and white beans, plus spaghetti (no other kind of pasta) with various meat-based sauces, and grilled meat.

and the peppery Bordeaux-style "Tzingana" are produced from impeccably farmed vines. Biodynamic sprays of fermented cow manure aerated in water are dripped on the vineyard topsoils, giving them a more friable texture. This allows rain water to penetrate more easily and to prevent soil erosion, a perennial problem in hot regions like Chianti where rain tends to fall in short, sharp bursts. And elegance in the wine is preserved by soaking the grape skins in the chilled juice for a day or so before fermentation begins, allowing vital colour and flavour to be extracted but without too much extra tannin that would make the wine unwieldy. You can rent rooms here, or even the whole beautifully furnished house.

In the footsteps of Michelangelo

From Monte Bernardi turn right towards San Donato in Poggio for the Casavecchia alla Piazza (see p.57), where Valeria Sodano and Gabriele Buondonno (both agronomists from Naples) produce very refined organic Chianti, bursting with moreish, earthy plum flavours, a Syrah, called "Campo ai Ciliegi" notable for a very restrained level of alcohol (young Syrah vines can burn out on Chianti's hot, loose sandy soils), and one of Chianti's most sippable grappas. The estate used to belong to Michelangelo's family in the 15th century.

South of San Donato in Poggio at Isole you'll find the de Marchi family's Fattoria Isole e Olena, source of crisp but creamy Chardonnay, pinpoint reds like "L'Eremo" (Tuscany's first varietal Syrah, made from vines grafted onto Canaiolo in the mid-1980s as the fashion for Rhône varietals was about to take off), the fine-grained 100% Sangiovese "Cepparello", and total benchmark Chianti Classico, plus bitingly authentic vin santo. The vin santo barrels are dotted around the winery courtyard, creating extra complexity as each spot has its own humidity and temperature level, causing the fermenting yeast to work at different speeds during the three to six years it takes them to make the wines stable. The name Isole e Olena comes from the uniting of two hamlets, around which the vineyards are situated. One of these, Olena, is now almost deserted, and you could easily get lost in the courtyards of old houses now strewn with blue, yellow, and pink wild flowers.

Machiavellian option

From San Donato in Poggio join the dual carriageway at the San Donato exit, leaving at the San Casciano Sud exit. In San Casciano in Val di Pesa the Chianti Classico and Colli Fiorentini zones (*see* Florence chapter) meet. In San Casciano you could take the easy option and head straight toward a tourist trap like the Machiavelli winery (tel: 055 828471), former residence of Nicolò Machiavelli when he was exiled from Florence and where he wrote his famous work *The Prince*, but you'd be wiser to favour instead the likes of Fattoria Poggiopiano (*see* p.44).

Here brothers Stefano and Alessandro Bartoli use a mix of stainless steel, barrels, and wooden vats to good effect when softening their increasingly elegant reds. This is one of the few Chianti estates to shun Cabernet Sauvignon, partly, says Alessandro, because they want their Chiantis to taste of Sangiovese's red plum and not of Cabernet's blackcurrants, but also because the vineyards here are mainly north-facing, which makes it harder for Cabernet to ripen (unripe Cabernet smells leafy and peppery). The family also breeds black roosters of the famous Livorno breed of chicken.

ABOVE *Madonna, keeping watch.*

LEFT *Wild flowers in spring.*

Around San Casciano
Other good wineries in San Casciano include the Ponticelli brothers' Il Mandorlo (tel: 055 8228211; info@il-mandorlo.it) for its showy Sangiovese/Cabernet blend "Terrato"; Carlo Cattaneo's Massanera winery (www.massanera.com), partly for its unusually soft wines but also for the animals like pigs, ducks, rabbits, and pigeons that can be served in the winery restaurant; and the Castelli del Grevepesa cooperative (tel: 055 821911; info@castellidelgrevepesa.it) on Via Grevigiana, where some of the lowest prices of Chianti wines are found in the on-site shop (the co-op also ships wines to the UK and USA).

Head back to Florence on the back roads, via Impruneta by way of Mercatale in Val di Pesa, where Fattoria Ispoli (*see* p.44; by appointment; English spoken) is found. Clay-rich, limey soils here help retain water in the hottest years and give the fruit flavours in the local red wines a perceptible spine of acidity. Ispoli's rich, unfiltered Chianti reds, in which the Sangiovese is softened with low-yield Merlot, are complemented by super-concentrated olive oils. Also in Mercatale Val di Pesa is Villa Branca (tel: 055 821033; www.villabranca.it; call ahead for a cellar tour) where Chianti Classicos are aged in barrels of American oak prepared by French barrel-makers to give the wines' red fruit flavours a coconut-style veneer. There are also self-contained apartments here for rental.

Route Two: Chianti south
From southeast of the railway station in Siena find the SS408 to Ponte a Bozzone. Turn left on the road to the hamlets of Pontignanello and Pontignano and the first winery signposted

ABOVE *Tying the vines to stakes.*

RIGHT *A room with a view.*

WHERE TO STAY

Castello di Meleto
Loc Meleto
53013 Gaiole in Chianti (SI)
Tel: 0577 749129/217
www.castellomeleto.it
Six holiday flats with
private gardens under
the castle walls, plus
communal pool and wine
bar. Bed and breakfast
accommodation in a former
parsonage also available.

Montegiachi
SP62 no 35, 53019
Castelnuovo Berardenga (SI)
Tel: 0577 363091
www.montegiachi.com
Two roomy, secluded
farmhouses with satellite
TV on an estate owned
by the same family for
over six centuries.

on the left is Tenuta di Monaciano (*see* p.49). The main villa contains wide-ranging flower- and fountain-filled grounds first laid out in the 19th century, with statues, aviaries (including one for peacocks) plus a *limonaia* or lemon-house. Just before you reach Pontignanello is Paolo and Pietro Losi's Querciavalle (tel: 0577 356842; az.agricolalosi@libero.it; by appointment), which has some beautifully sited southwest-facing Chianti Classico vineyards, and good value wines, too.

Generations of wine

Carry on through Pontignano to the T-junction with the SP102 and head right (north) to the hamlet of Vagliagli, passing Elena and Mario Gallo's Fattoria di Corsignano (*see* p.49), whose rose- and lavender-filled vineyards afford clear views of Siena, just 8km (5 miles) away. Pass the no-frills Vigna al Sole (tel: 0577 322694) to reach Sandro Bandini's Oliviera, which has been in the same family for five generations (not to be confused with the nearby Poggio dell'Oliviera owned by another branch of the Bandini clan).

Tourist package

Continue to Vagliagli, passing signposts for Borgo Scopeto (www.caparzo.com) on the right, the Chianti Classico outpost of Elisabetta Gnudi Angelini, who also owns Tenuta Caparzo and Altesino in Montalcino (*see* p.107).

In Vagliagli itself you'll find the Fattoria di Dievole (*see* p.53, an estate transformed over the last 15 years from a near ruin to one of Chianti's most marketable and visitor-friendly wineries. Dievole's wines, such as the Chianti Classico "Novecento" and the new oak barrel-aged 100% Sangiovese red "Broccato", are well distributed in restaurants throughout Tuscany and are made in an easy-to-appreciate rather than complex style, with crisp fruit flavours very evident due to the relatively low-lying, valleyed nature of the vineyards. The Dievole complex features a hotel (double rooms and suites), plus holiday villas in converted farmhouses across the estate. Dievole also offers restaurant and bar facilities, a wellness and sports centre, conference and seminar rooms, and even a honeymoon complex.

Historic wineries

As you leave Vagliagli on the road towards Radda in Chianti, Fattoria della Aiola (see p.53) appears on the right. The estate is a fortified villa-cum-castle dating from the 13th century, and was bought by the father of the current owners, the Malogodi family, in the 1960s. A solid range of wines is produced, including a dry white Val d'Arbia Bianco, Chianti Classico, the Sangiovese "Rosso del Senatore", the Cabernet/Sangiovese red "Logaiolo", and a decent vin santo.

Continue towards Radda in Chianti, passing Fattoria di Terrabianca (www.terrabianca.com), owned by the reliable Roberto Guldener. The top wines here are the "Ceppate" Cabernet Sauvignon, for its clear blackcurrant fruit, typical of this grape variety, and the Chianti Classico Riserva "Vigna della Croce" for its leafy red fruit.

Nearer Radda in Chianti, at the hamlet of San Giusto in Salcio, turn right on the SP114 in the direction of Lecchi in Chianti, then right again on the SS408 for the hamlet of Pianella. In Pianella look for the SP9 road to Canonica a Cerreto. Here the Lorenzi family produces generously thick red wines from hand-picked grapes, which offer good value, too. The estate is a former abbey, built around 1000AD by the canons of Siena's cathedral, and you can stay in rooms once used by the monks, now converted into modern apartments that offer fantastic views across unspoilt countryside.

Banking on a good vintage

From Pianella hamlet head to Castelnuovo Berardenga via the hamlet of Barca on the SP62. Continue past the wine estate of Montegiachi (see box, left) to reach Poggio Bonelli (www.poggiobonelli.it), owned by Siena's most powerful bank, the Monte dei Paschi di Siena, which was founded in 1472. As you would expect from an estate owned by bankers, winemaking is done very much by the book, leading to a safe and reliable rather than exciting Chianti Classico. A newly

WHERE TO EAT

Ristorante La Bottega del 30 [A1]
Loc Villa a Sesta
Via Santa Caterina, 2
53019 Castelnuovo
Berardenga (SI)
Tel: 0577 359226
www.labottegadel30.it
Closed Tuesday and Wednesday. Owned by Villa a Sesta winery. Reservation requested (only 30 seats). Homemade bread, huge selection of antipasti, with signature dish roast shin of veal, marinated in milk.

Ristorante di Pietrafitta [C3]
Loc Pietrafitta
53011 Castellina in Chianti (SI)
Tel: 0577 741123
Closed Tuesday. Lamb and beef specialist, with home-made pasta and plenty of fresh vegetables in a modern Tuscan style.

WHERE TO EAT

Osteria al Ponte [C2]
Loc Rocca di Castagnoli
Via A. Casabianca, 25
53013 Gaiole in Chianti (SI)
Tel: 0577 744007
Closed Monday. Smoked
tuna; *bruschetta* with
tomato, mushrooms, and
basil; garlic soup; veal
with capers and *rucola*.

**Ristorante Enoteca
al Gallopapa [C3]**
Via delle Volte, 14/16
53011 Castellina
in Chianti (SI)
Tel: 0577 742939
www.gallopapa.com
Closed Thursday. Stylish
eatery offers sheep's cheese
with pumpkin, walnuts,
and red onion; rabbit
with fennel and tomato
confit; saffron risotto with
asparagus; pigeon breast
with cocoa beans, mashed
potato, and garlic purée.

BELOW *The inevitable winery
cats, to keep pests under control.*

created barrel-aged red called "Tramonto d'Oca", from 80%
Sangiovese and 20% Merlot, first made in 2000, could herald
a new, more dynamic era here.

In Castelnuovo Berardenga find the SN484 road north
towards San Gusme in Chianti, and just as you leave
Castelnuovo, after the huge stone wall of the churchyard,
you'll see Fattoria di Felsina (Berardenga) signposted on
the left (*see* box, right; by appointment). In fact the cellars
are technically just outside the Chianti Classico sub-zone,
but Felsina's vineyards are inside it. Owner Giuseppe
Mazzacolin is a university intellectual turned winemaker, and
he is equally happy discussing literature (Italian and English-
language) as he is the way the soil changes subtly from this,
the most southerly part of the Chianti Classico zone, to the
most northerly part of the Chianti Colli Senesi zone
immediately to the south.

In fact, Mazzacolin has an estate in Chianti Senesi called
Castello di Farnetella, whose excellent quality and value-for-
money wines you can taste here. Felsina Berardenga's range
includes a delicious dry white barrel-fermented Chardonnay
called "I Sistri", a bright, creamy, and elegant *vin santo* made
from Malvasia, Trebbiano, and Sangiovese (hence a slightly
amber colour). For the reds he has a 100% Cabernet
Sauvignon called "Maestro Raro", named after a musical work
by Robert Schumann, with sweet-tasting chocolate tannin
and blackcurrant fruit; classic Chianti Classico; Chianti Classico
Riserva "Vigneto Rancia" showing clear fruit and smooth
textures; plus "Fontalloro", a 100% Sangiovese whose flavours
of new oak are quietly assembled behind characteristic bitter
cherry fruit. The cellars are impressive, with one part lying
underneath a former grain store, a reminder of when the largest
Tuscan estates were self-sufficient mixed farms.

International appeal
Continue along the SS484 to San Gusme in Chianti and Villa
Arceno (*see* box, right) is signposted on the right. The
controlling interest here is held by California wine producer
Kendall-Jackson after a plan to turn the estate into holiday
homes fell through. Not surprisingly the wines are made to
suit the international American, rather than classic European,
palate, with juicy, rather than more austere, fruit textures key.
Hence the vineyards are dominated by the Merlot grape, which
ripens early and gives much softer, juicier wines than the Tuscan
Sangiovese, which can be aggressive. The visitor facilities here
are clean, cool, and airy.

From San Gusme stay on the SS484, direction Gaiole in
Chianti, passing the vineyards and olive groves of Villa a' Sesta.
There is a restaurant here called La Bottega del 30 (*see* p.51),

and Villa a Sesta also owns a rather exclusive hotel and polo club near Bucine in Arezzo province.

The next winery signposted on the left is San Felice (www.agricolasanfelice.it), one of the most historically renowned names in Chianti Classico but, on the evidence of today's wine quality and despite recent improvements, it is fair to say that San Felice is famous for being famous.

A mixed blessing

The next winery of note on the SS484, just before the hamlet of San Regolo, is the Castello di Brolio (see box, right; free daily cellar tours 9am–6pm weekdays and Saturdays in summer; fee payable to see the gardens and the castle). The estate is now under the control of the 32nd generation of the noble Ricasoli family. In the late 19th century Baron Bettino Ricasoli (1809–80), who served as Italy's second Prime Minister in the formative years after Italian unification, was also responsible for recommending that Chianti red wines contained a proportion of white grapes. The original idea was a good one, especially as the acidity of the white grapes kept the wines fresher for longer; but poor clones of Sangiovese lacking colour were planted in the 1960s and, for growers opting for rather high grape yields, the addition of white grapes began to make no sense, so the Chianti regulations were finally changed in the 1990s.

The Brolio vineyards contain over 250 viziati or so-called "spoiled" vines planted in conjunction with local universities and the Chianti wine-growers' consortium. These "spoiled" grapes were once used in Chianti Classico but were discarded, with names like Palle di Gatto ("cat's balls"), Strozzaprete ("priest strangler"), Igannacane, Tinturie, Pisciancione, and Boggiole. Those showing the most promise may be reintroduced.

Castello di Brolio's range of wines has improved after a very poor period before the mid-1990s, and offers soft, juicy, and very lightly flavoured Chianti Classico reds and the oaky "Casalferro" Sangiovese. There is also a restored farmhouse hidden in woodland at Brolio with several independent self-catering apartments for rental.

Family connections

From Brolio carry on towards Gaiole in Chianti and you'll soon see the Castello di Cacchiano (tel: 0557 747018; cacchiano@chianticlassico.com), owned by another branch of the Ricasoli family, the Baroni Ricasoli-Firidolfi. It dates from the 10th century, and produces slightly firmer and arguably more authentic wines than the Castello di Brolio. There is also a manor house for rental featuring a swimming pool in a well-designed sunken garden.

WINERIES IN CHIANTI SOUTH

Canonica a Cerreto [A1]
Fraz Vagliagli
53019 Castelnuovo
Berardenga (SI)
Tel: 0577 363261
www.canonicacerreto.it

Castello di Brolio [C2]
Loc Brolio
53013 Gaiole
in Chianti (SI)
Tel: 0577 7301
shop@ricasoli.it
www.ricasoli.it

Fattoria della Aiola [A1]
Fraz Vagliagli
53010 Castelnuovo
Berardenga (SI)
Tel: 0577 322615
aiola@chianticlassico.com

Fattoria di Dievole [A1]
Fraz Vagliagli
Loc Dievole
53019 Castelnuovo
Berardenga (SI)
Tel: 0577 322613
www.dievole.it

Fattoria di Felsina [A1]
Via del Chianti, 101
53019 Castelnuovo
Berardenga (SI)
Tel: 0577 355117
felsina@dada.it

Fattoria di Terrabianca [C2]
Loc San Fedele a Paterno
53017 Radda
in Chianti (SI)
Tel: 0577 54029
www.terrabianca.com

Riecine [C2]
Loc Riecine
53013 Gaiole
in Chianti (SI)
Tel: 0577 749098
www.riecine.com

Villa Arceno [B1]
Loc Arceno
53010 San Gusme (SI)
Tel: 0577 359346
www.arceno.it

RIGHT *A shady spot to shelter from the midday sun.*

BELOW RIGHT *Sheep dot Chianti's fields. Local lamb is a good match for the wine.*

WINERIES IN CHIANTI SOUTH (CONTINUED)

Badia a Coltibuono [C2]
Loc Badia a Coltibuono
53013 Gaiole in Chianti (SI)
Tel: 0577 74481
www.coltibuono.com

Casina di Cornia [C3]
Loc Cornia 113
53011 Castellina
in Chianti (SI)
Tel: 0577 743052
www.casinadicornia.com

Castagnoli [C3]
Loc Castagnoli, 53011
Castellina in Chianti (SI)
Tel: 0577 740446
castagnoli@valdelsa.net

Castello di Fonterùtoli [C3]
Loc Fonterùtoli
Via Ottone III, 5
53011 Castellina
in Chianti (SI)
Tel: 0577 73571
www.fonterutoli.it

Le Miccine [C2]
SS Traversa Chiantigiana
53013 Gaiole in Chianti (SI)
Tel: 0577 749526
www.lemiccine.com

Rocca della Macìe [C3]
Loc Macìe, 53011
Castellina in Chianti (SI)
Tel: 0577 7321
www.roccadellemacie.com

Tenuta Caparsa [C2]
Loc Caparsino, 48
53017 Radda in Chianti (SI)
Tel: 0577 738174
www.caparsa.it

A little further on the Castello di Tornano (www.castelloditornano.it), which is signposted on the left, offers farmhouse accommodation, horse-riding with an instructor, and a cookery school run by an established local chef who will take you to local markets to search out the freshest produce before guiding you in the estate's kitchens for hands-on tuition in groups of no more than six people.

South of Gaiole in Chianti the huge Agricoltori del Chianti Geografico (www.chiantigeografico.it) wine cooperative is signposted, a good place to fill up on cheap party wines. If you follow the road east to the medieval fortified *borgo* of Castagnoli you pass Castello di Meleto (*see* p.50), the Rietine estate (www.rietine.com), which is sometimes confused with Riecine (*see* below). Then you'll find the Rocca di Castagnoli (www.roccadicastagnoli.com) winery, with its own restaurant, the Osteria al Ponte (*see* p.52) and rooms to rent named after the trades practised at Castagnoli in medieval times: Bottaio (cooper), Fornaciaio (kilnsman), Mugnaio (miller), Funaio (ropemaker), Carraio (wheelwright), and Fabbro (blacksmith). Wines include an easy-drinking white called "Molino delle Balze", along with Cabernet-, Merlot-, and Sangiovese-based reds showing subtle varietal character.

A cool customer

Leave the SP408 through Gaiole in Chianti by following the small track behind the town's southeastern corner to Riecine (see p.53), run by the reflective Sean O'Callaghan. The vineyards are dotted around Gaiole in Chianti, and are easily spotted by the profusion of wild grasses and flowers that are allowed to grow between the vine rows. Sean O'Callaghan studied winemaking in Germany, where long, cool fermentations are the norm for white wines. Riecine makes only reds, and cooler than normal fermentations preserve the floral flavours (peony and tulip) in the Sangiovese grape, which dominates Riecine's vineyards, notably in the delicious peony- and tulip-flavoured 100% Sangiovese "La Gioia".

Cook up a feast

Carry on up the track from Riecine, crossing over the SS429 Radda–Montevarchi road and into the forest for Badia a Coltibuono (see box, left). On the way in you pass Badia a Coltibuono's Osteria, a tavern selling the estate's wines, olive oil, and vinegar. Badia a Coltibuono's name means "Abbey of the Good Harvest" for it was founded in 1051 by monks who terraced the land for crop-growing and developed one of the earliest forms of tenant farming. You can stay here on a bed and breakfast basis in the monks' cells, which have been sensitively restored. They offer panoramic views across Chianti. Badia a Coltibuono also runs one of Tuscany's most admired cookery schools (see p.37), which offers one- and five-day courses that are very much hands-on. You can pick many of the ingredients to be used in the estate's own vegetable, fruit, and herb garden. The wines offer good value for money and come from vineyards located near Monti in Chianti (here it is too cool) where there is also a modern winery, which you can tour by prior appointment.

Around Radda

Turn back from Badia a Coltibuono, west along the SS429 to Radda in Chianti. On the left you'll pass the 16th-century Castello San Donato in Perano (see box, right). The wine style here from the estate's relatively young vineyards is evolving, but the restaurant and wine shop selling local wines and condiments are well worth a visit.

Further towards Radda the SP2 road is signed to the left, along

(see p.53)

WHERE TO EAT

Castello San Donato in Perano [C2]
Loc Perano
53013 Gaiole in Chianti (SI)
Tel: 0577 735635
www.castellosandonato.it
Classy restaurant with a terrace offering great views. There's a taverna downstairs for less formal fare.

Nerbone di Greve [E3]
Piazza Matteotti, 22
50022 Greve in Chianti (SI)
Tel: 055 853308
Closed Tuesday. Try the zucchini risotto, leek and potato soup, and lampredotto (similar to tripe, but thinnner and flatter – boiled with carrots and onions), and pappa al pomodoro.

Ristorante Carloni [C2]
Via G. Puccini, 24
53013 Gaiole in Chianti (SI)
Tel: 0577 749549
Friendly trattoria offering grilled meats, salt cod, and la panzanella (tomato and basil salad with wetted, stale bread and tomatoes).

WHERE TO EAT

Badia a Coltibuono [C2]
Loc Badia a Coltibuono
53013 Gaiole in Chianti (SI)
Tel: 0577 749424
ristbadia@coltibuono.com
Closed Monday in summer.
Simple but creative
seasonal Tuscan food based
on fresh ingredients grown
partly on the estate, with
lighter bistro food served
between lunch and dinner.

Pizzeria Il Bivacco [A1]
Loc Colonna del Grillo, 5
53019 Castelnuovo
Berardenga (SI)
Tel: 0577 352009
Popular with locals
for quick service and
reasonably priced pizzas,
salads, and hot snacks.

which is the tiny vineyard, olive grove, orchard, and vegetable garden of the Italo-American Weaver family's Le Miccine (*see* p.54; by appointment). You can rent part of the owner's 300-year-old house by the week – and guests get discounts on the wine. Dry and sweet whites, plus Chianti Classico reds, are made in a generous style, and Le Miccine's English-speaking staff are very helpful, with informative, fun cellar tours.

If you want to explore north of Radda (follow the SP112), head to the Castello di Volpaia (tel: 0577 738066; www.volpaia.com; visits by appointment) which dominates the fortified village or *borgo* of Volpaia. The style of Chianti here is quite soft, thanks to loose-textured sandy soils which encourage early grape ripening. Accommodation is on offer, consisting of plush apartments available to rent by the week.

Cooling off
Our route takes us on a right-hand turn just west of Radda onto the SP2 for Tenuta Caparsa (*see* p.54). The vineyards are relatively cool, and north-facing, one benefit of which is that heat-loving pests like the red spider mite (who like to make their homes in the bark of the vine trunks) are much rarer here than in the warmer, lower-lying vineyards. Caparsa's owner Paolo Cianferoni makes beautifully pure reds tasting of wet earth and hedgerow fruits.

Carry on from Radda to Castellina in Chianti along the SS429, where west of the town off the SP130 you'll find Castagnoli (see p.54), not to be confused with Rocca di Castagnoli in Gaiole. Here Hans Joachim Dobbelin makes incredibly ethereal Syrah, Merlot, and Sangiovese reds from vineyards enjoying cool nights and cooling breezes due to their altitude. They are grown at over 400 metres (1,312 feet), when around 350 metres (1,148 feet) is the Chianti norm. Don't be put off by the apparent lightness of colour in these red wines, especially since Sangiovese is not the world's most highly charged grape colour-wise.

From Castellina turn south onto the SS222 or the "Chiantigiana" road. In the centre of Castellina in Chianti take the right-hander onto the SP51 for Rocca delle Macìe (see p.54), whose extensive vineyards produce one of Chianti Classico's most recognizable brands in an easy, lightly flavoured style. You can enjoy free wine tastings in Rocca delle Macìe's winery shop (tel: 0577 732236; open daily), which also sells the estate's honey and olive oil, or stay in Rocca delle Macìe's hotel, the Relais Riserva di Fizzano, with restaurant (www.riservadifizzano.com), which is located in a restored medieval village.

Border disputes

Carry on south from Castellina to reach the hamlet of Fonterùtoli and the immense Castello di Fonterùtoli (see p.54). The 1208 Treaty of Fonterùtoli determined the boundary between Siena and Florence, two communities perpetually at war. Legend has it that two horsemen were supposed to gallop at dawn from their respective cities, with their meeting point determining the official boundary. However, the Florentine rooster, hungry at being deliberately underfed by its crafty Florentine owners crowed earlier than its Sienese peer, hence Florence's territory is the larger. The story is remembered by the black rooster symbol adorning the wines of Chianti Classico. Fonterùtoli has its own wine store from which tours of the ultra-modern cellars begin, with conical fermentation vats for Chianti reds to give them extra colour by allowing more of the fermenting wine to stay in contact with the colour-containing grape skins for longer.

Leave Fonterùtoli and take the first main right-hander onto the SP119 until you reach Quatrostrade, a crossroads where you turn right for Casina di Cornia (see p.54), where Antoine Luginbühl and Francine Dufour produce one of the best organic Chianti Classicos. You can stay in a converted haybarn (open all year round) and admire views over hayfields, plus there is Francine's pottery workshop in which the glazings are made from the prunings of the vines and the olive trees.

Take the SS222 to return to Siena.

WHERE TO STAY

Casavecchia alla Piazza
Loc Casavecchia
alla Piazza, 37
53011 Castellina
in Chianti (SI)
Tel: 0577 749754
www.buondonno.com
Welcoming guesthouse amid rambling olive groves with extensive views. English spoken.

Fattoria di Rignana
Via di Rignana, 15
50022 Panzano in Chianti (FI)
Tel: 055 852065
www.rignana.it
Stunning villa with 11th-century origins. Single rooms, bed and breakfast, or an apartment or whole house to rent (eight double rooms). Good wine, too.

Podere Collelungo
Loc Collelungo, 53011
Castellina in Chianti (SI)
Tel: 0577 740489
www.collelungo.com
Eleven cosy, sought-after apartments in isolated location, plus fun bar serving Collelungo's own fruity Chiantis.

Relais Vignale [C2]
Via XX Settembre
53017 Radda in Chianti (SI)
Tel: 0577 738300
www.vignale.it
Charming hotel plus restaurant and wine bar, with terraced views over the vineyard. Famous for being where the Chianti Classico boundaries were officially signed in 1924.

LEFT *Cover crops between the rows provide a colourful habitat for friendly insects.*

Chianti Rufina and Pomino

If you find the heat and humidity of Florence on the Arno Valley floor oppressive, you should head east and up into the cooler, more airy confines of the Sieve Valley. This runs right into Italy's mountainous spine, the Apennines, providing on the way the robust slopes of the Chianti region's most highly regarded sub-zone, Rufina.

Ancient history

Within Rufina is the Pomino region, which was recognized as far back as 1716 in Cosimo Medici III's Tuscan vineyard register and today is better known for its dry white wines than its reds. The cold air running from the Apennines down to the Mediterranean gives the red wines of Rufina and Pomino a gentle, crisp freshness and a capacity to age longer than the average Chianti. The crispness is gentle because the slopes are well-exposed southeast and southwest to the sun. A combination of cold air and altitudes of up to 600 metres (1,968 feet) in the highest vineyards means ripening is late for the red Sangiovese grape. This can make for slightly bitter wines, but does also mean extra complexity from extended ripening. The coolness means that white wines, especially in Pomino, should retain their aroma, flavour, and elegance even after two or three years in bottle.

Distinguishing wines

The best producers, like the Giuntinis of Selvapiana, believe that when Rufina was incorporated into the greater Chianti region (in 1932) it lost its identity. This is true in the sense that the larger producers, such as Villa di Vetrice and the huge merchant Ruffino (www.ruffino.com), which is based in Pontassieve, churn out Chiantis and Chianti Rufinas which are largely indistinguishable from each other, confusing wine buyers. Stick with the smaller producers recommended here if you like your Chianti Rufinas to have the lip-sticking bite of mountain-fresh air.

There are less than 50 producers in Pomino and Rufina, and tasting rooms can get crowded in summer with day-trippers from Florence, so book ahead if you really want to explore the wine cellars, many of which have been modernized over the last decade. Travelling around the zone by car is fairly easy, as signposting is good, and even in the hilliest areas the roads are well maintained. The only slight blot is the ugly town of Pontassieve, which spoils the foreground when you look from the head of the Sieve Valley back down towards Florence.

Getting there
By car Rufina is 24km (15 miles) east of Florence on the SS67 Florence–Pontassieve–Dicomano road. There is a regular railway service to Pontassieve from Florence's Santa Maria Novella station. Local bus services are run by SITA.

Travelling around
Route summary The route takes us from Florence to Pontassieve, up the Sieve Valley to Rufina and Scopeti for the right-hand turn to Pomino, then Borselli where you head back to Florence along the Arno's south bank, via the Chianti Colli Fiorentini *comune* of Bagno a Ripoli. The route is about 72km (45 miles). Allow two days.

Route: Rufina and Pomino
From Florence take the SS67 along the north bank of the Arno to Pontassieve for Fattoria I Veroni (*see* p.61), which is on the right of the town as you enter from Florence. I Veroni means "a place where tobacco is dried". Owner Lorenzo Mariani's family bought the estate in the 19th century, when the terraces along the banks of the Arno were used to grow tobacco and grain. Mariani has reconstituted the oldest vineyards and planted new ones on gentle slopes. Relics of a bygone era remain in the form of 60- and 70-year-old vines trained up fruit trees instead of wooden posts. Simple but firm Chianti Rufina reds offering reasonable value are produced, plus softer reds like "Pelacane" from Merlot and Syrah with a bit of Petit Verdot and a caramel-like *vin santo*.

Also in Pontassieve, but on the slopes overlooking the town above the Arno's north bank, is Fattoria Cerreto Libri (*see* p.61). The vineyards here are some of the best in the zone – Selvapiana rented them for a time in the mid-1990s when it was looking to invest in a small neighbouring vineyard called "Erchi". This is the warmest part of the Rufina zone due to its relatively low altitude, so full ripeness of the grapes is usually assured.

Chianti Rufina and Pomino
Florence (Chianti Colli Fiorentini) and Montespertoli
Route: Rufina and Pomino
Allow two days

RIGHT *Selvapiana winery produces old-vine Chianti Rufina Riserva and legendary vin santo.*

Fattoria Cerreto Libri is a rambling, 18th-century farm. Owner Valentina Baldini's father established the vines here in the 1970s, and she is now moving her olives and vines from organics to Biodynamics. Biodynamic growers try to time agricultural work to lunar phases, such as ploughing weeds away when the moon is in Leo so the weed seeds don't re-germinate (try it in your garden). The red wines have become much cleaner recently thanks to better picking and winery hygiene, with elegant, fine-grained Chianti Rufina (the *riserva* still needs some work) and a blend of Sangiovese and Canaiolo called "Podernuovo". There is also atmospheric accommodation to rent.

From Pontassieve you can access two interesting producers by staying on the western side of the Sieve River on the Via di Montefiesole for Fattoria Lavacchio (tel: 055 8317472; info@fattorialavacchio.com). It has an old windmill, a working olive press, and what look like excellent newly planted vineyards, with grape varieties including Chardonnay. Keep going on the same road, but turn left back to Florence for the genteel Marchese Gondi's old-style reds from Tenuta di Bossi.

Our route, however, from Pontassieve takes us up the eastern bank of the Sieve on the SS67, direction Dicomano.

After 5km (3 miles), turn right over the railway crossing for Selvapiana (see box, right). This is one of the best producers in the entire Chianti zone, and way out front in terms of quality in the microcosm of Chianti Rufina. It is now run by the laid back Federico Masseti, who dropped out of his farming studies at the University of Florence to come and learn in a more practical way, on the land. He ended up at Selvapiana, and after a few years' work he was adopted by Selvapiana's owner, the heirless Francesco Giuntini.

Now Federico Giuntini-Masseti (as he has become known) is building a new cellar, expanding Selvapiana's vineyards, and considering the switch from certified organic farming to Biodynamics. The oldest vines in the single-vineyard Chianti Rufina Riserva "Bucerchiale" produce a powerful, but enormously refreshing red with wild fruit and cedar flavours. Giuntini-Masseti is taking cuttings from these old vines for the next generation of Selvapiana vineyards. The estate's vin santo is legendary for its consistency and mouth-watering freshness, and Selvapiana's honeys and olive oils deservedly grace some of the world's finest restaurant tables.

High-altitude vines

Continue up the SS37 past Rufina town towards Dicomano. At the right-hand turn for Pomino you pass the small, young, but potentially forward-thinking Perini family's estate of Lecciole (www.ilpezzatino.it). If you keep going to Dicomano and take the left-hand turn to the Colognole estate, you'll reach one of the highest vineyards in the zone (see box, left).

Instead turn right to Pomino at Lecciole, and the landscape becomes much tighter as the road narrows through woodland interspersed with vineyards. You pass the winery and vineyards of Fattoria Petrognano, which Selvapiana now rents, but you can stay here, too (see box, left).

Continue into Pomino, a small farming village, dominated by the vineyards of Florence-based merchant Frescobaldi, at Castello di Pomino. The high altitude, of up to 650 metres (2,132 feet), makes for crisp wines, in a clean, direct style, like the Chardonnay-based "Il Benefizio". Reds are trickier, as the grapes can taste underripe, adding a lettuce-leaf note to the fruit. Part of the problem is that rules for Pomino Rosso require 15–25% of the late-ripening Bordeaux grape Cabernet Sauvignon. It is included in Pomino due to an accident of history. In the 16th century local landowners, the Albizis, were exiled to France by the Medicis. When they returned in the 18th century, they brought French grapes with them. Frescobaldi acquired vineyards here by marriage into the Albizi family in 1887.

WINERIES IN CHIANTI RUFINA AND POMINO

PRICES: moderate to expensive

Fattoria Cerreto Libri [A3]
Via Aretina, 90
50056 Pontassieve (FI)
Tel: 055 8314528
fattoria@cerretolibri.it
www.cerretolibri.it

Fattoria Lavacchio [A3]
Via di Montefiesole, 55
50065 Pontassieve (FI)
Tel: 055 8317472
info@fattorialavacchio.com

Fattoria Selvapiana [A3]
Loc Selvapiana, 43
50065 Pontassieve (FI)
Tel: 055 8369848
selvapiana@tin.it
www.selvapiana.it

Fattoria I Veroni [A3]
Via Tifariti, 5
50065 Pontassieve (FI)
Tel: 055 8368886
info@iveroni.it
www.iveroni.it

Petreto [A3]
Via di Rosano, 196/A
50012 Pontassieve (FI)
Tel: 055 6519021

Travignoli [A2]
Via Travignoli, 78
50060 Pelago (FI)
Tel: 055 8361098
info@travignoli.com
www.travignoli.com

ABOVE *Villages and vines clinging to the hills of the Sieve Valley.*

WHERE TO EAT

Ristorante Degli Artisti [C2]
Piazza Romagnoli, 1
50032 Borgo San Lorenzo (FI)
Tel: 055 457707
Closed on Wednesday.
Try lamb with garlic and anchovies, boar with nuts and raisins, ravioli stuffed with cauliflower in truffle and mascarpone sauce, and hot apple pastries.

Ristorante La Casa Del Prosciutto [C2]
Via Ponte A. Vicchio, 1
50039 Vicchio (FI)
Tel: 055 844031
Simple but reliable food, like ricotta and spinach balls or *ribollita* bread soup with seasonal mushrooms.

Carry on towards the hamlet of Borselli for Frescobaldi's Castello di Nipozzano (www.frescobaldi.it) on the right, which produces Chianti Rufina. This wine starts life firm and peppery to taste, but develops tan and leather flavours after three years in bottle. Frescobaldi's top Chianti Rufina, "Remole", also needs a couple of years for the oak flavours to soften and harmonize.

One small producer of note here is Travignoli (see p.61), whose vineyards enjoy good southeast-facing slopes and produce good value-for-money wines. There is a quaint tasting room, an underground cellar, and nice views, too.

Head back to Pontassieve by turning left onto the SP70, but cross south over the Arno onto the Via di Rosano (direction Florence) for Petreto (see p.61), on the left-hand side just before a garden nursery. Owner Alessandro Fonseca has a genial way with words and has made a name for a late-picked white wine called "Pourriture Noble" (French for "noble rot"). This is made in the same way as Bordeaux's Sauternes, and from similar grapes (Semillon and Sauvignon Blanc). River mists from the Arno shrivel the grapes in late autumn as the noble rot fungus *Botrytis cinerea* settles on the skins, making for soft, honey-sweet white wines, quite distinctive from most *vin santos*. Petreto's red wines are very gentle in style, with oak flavours well in the background, with the 100% Merlot "Bocciolé" a good example.

Florence

Florence's romantic architecture hides its fearsome political power, based on the city being one of the birthplaces of banking from the Middle Ages onwards. In wine terms Florence is the home of Tuscany's, and one of Italy's, most powerful winemaking families. The Antinoris (*see* p.64) have been in the wine business in Florence since 1385 and have vineyards in all the major Tuscan regions (Ornellaia in Bolgheri on the Etruscan coast; Pian delle Vigne in Montalcino) and in other parts of Italy, too.

Super Tuscany

Antinori's visitor-friendly Florence headquarters includes a wine bar-restaurant and a shop where you can buy Antinori's famous Super Tuscans like Ornellaia and Tignanello. Adherents say these wines broke the mould of Tuscan reds by blending foreign Bordeaux grapes with the Chianti staple Sangiovese; some critics feel, however, that these famous blends can exhibit something of a southern Mediterranean feel, such as their softness, and are neither "super" nor "Tuscan", nor even individual enough to merit their high prices.

Being such a political place, it is no surprise that the borders of the zone for Chianti from Florence's hills (or Chianti Colli Fiorentini denomination) are a political creation: the best parts, around San Casciano, can produce wine as good as neighbouring Chianti Classico; the flatter areas near the Arno can be some of the least benign for wine quality in Tuscany.

The hills to either side and south of Florence are marked by sometimes stark medieval castles and impressive, often Medici-inspired, villas as well as by the footprints of great men like Leonardo da Vinci, who hailed from here. Leonardo's birth place, Vinci, is home to the Florence wine cooperative (tel: 0571 902444; info@cantineleonardo.it). Sadly, its "Chianti Leonardo" and "Merlot degli Artisti" ("Artists' Merlot") brands do little credit either to the region or to Leonardo.

Traditionally all of the area's Chianti reds were styled for drinking in Florence's undemanding *trattorie*. Despite recent improvements to make Chianti Colli Fiorentini a more serious contender, this part of Tuscany still lacks a really outstanding wine estate that might persuade us that Florence really does deserve a better reputation.

Furthermore, the region's most influential contemporary domains have remained large (with well over 50 hectares of vines, not to mention huge olive groves) despite the break-up

LOCAL INFORMATION

APT (Agenzia per il Turismo) Firenze [D3]
Via A Manzoni, 16
50121 Firenze (FI)
Tel: 055 23320
info@firenzeturismo.it
www.firenzeturismo.it

Florence's very capable tourist office can help with wine enquiries. There are several other APT offices dotted around the city, too. Full details can be found on the website.

Comune di Montespertoli Ufficio Turismo [B4]
Piazza del Popolo, 1
50025 Montespertoli (FI)
Tel: 0571 6001

The address and phone number are that of the local tourist office.

WINERIES IN COLLI FIORENTINI AND MONTESPERTOLI

PRICES: generally moderate

Azienda Agricola Casale [A4]
Via San Martino-Casale, 150
50052 Certaldo (FI)
Tel: 0571 669262
casale@libero.it

**Azienda Agricola
Il Termine [C3]**
Loc Ferrone
Via delle Sodera, 47
50023 Impruneta (FI)
Tel: 055 207135/037/080
termine@ftbcc.it

**Fattoria San Michele
a Torri [D3]**
Via San Michele, 36
50020 Scandicci (FI)
Tel: 055 769111
sanmichele@dada.it
www.fattoriasanmichele.it

Fattoria Le Sorgenti [C2]
Loc Vallina
Via di Doccioloa, 8
50012 Bagno a Ripoli (FI)
Tel: 055 696004
info@fattoria-lesorgenti.com
www.fattoria-lesorgenti.com

Fattoria Torre a Cona [C1]
Loc San Donato in Collina
50010 Rignano Sull'Arno (FI)
Tel: 055 699000
info@villatorreacona.com
www.villatorreacona.com

Marchesi Antinori [D3]
Piazza degli Antinori, 3
50123 Firenze (FI)
Tel: 055 23595
antinori@antinori.it
www.antinori.it

**Tenuta San Vito
in Fior di Selva [C4]**
Via San Vito, 32
50056 Montelupo
Fiorentino (FI)
Tel: 0571 51411
sanvito@san-vito.com
www.san-vito.com

of the *mezzadria* sharecropping system in the 1960s. These estates often appear to be run by counts and barons who seem quite content to continue the aristocratic traditions of producing wine without necessarily thinking they need to update either their vineyard management or winemaking to make the kind of wines a more discerning public, rather than their ancestors, want to drink.

Many have several business activities (banking, industry, commerce, the law, politics) and employ external winemaking consultants whose often heavy-handed vineyard management and winemaking tricks with blending and oak barrels mask whatever typicity the grapes once had.

This is why most of the estates highlighted here as "wineries to visit" are the much smaller, more hands-on family-run concerns who are often organic or organically inclined. They are also, in the main, much more visitor-friendly than their aristocratic counterparts, producing vibrant Chiantis in which neither the fruit flavours nor the tannins of their Sangiovese grapes are forced by early picking (a problem to which the largest vineyards are especially prone) or the use of excessive oak to mask an inherent lack of flavour.

Time for change?
Some growers do, however, sense the need for change here, as elsewhere, so international grapes like Cabernet Sauvignon and Merlot (predictably), Syrah (sensibly), and Pinot Noir (ridiculously) intermingle with the still dominant Sangiovese.

One final word of caution: bottles from members of the Chianti Colli Fiorentini Consorzio (or consortium) bear as a logo the lion from the tower of the Palazzo Vecchio in Florence joined with the chalice of the Chianti Colli Fiorentini, but in most cases this symbol is no indication of any extra quality or consistency. The new (since 1998) sub-zone of Montespertoli in the west is another political creation rather than a recognition that this *comune* produces more distinctive wines than the rest of Florence's hills. But then Florence always has been a political place.

Getting there
Florence is easy to reach by car as it lies on the A1 autostrada from Bologna/Milan in the north and Rome to the south. The A1 intersects here with the A11 autostrada to Pisa. To reach Florence from Siena take the toll-free *"4 corsie"* or dual carriageway, the SP2. Florence is about two hours from Rome or one hour from Bologna on the Bologna–Rome train-line (www.trenitalia.it). Local bus services run by SITA (tel: 055 47821; www.sita-on-line.net) operate from Via Santa Caterina di Siena near the railway station.

Travelling around

Route summary The Colli Fiorentini zone is a half-moon shape. Our route follows the entire edge of this half-moon, in an anti-clockwise direction, beginning and ending in the city of Florence via Lastra a Signa, Montelupo Fiorentino, Montespertoli, Certaldo, Barberino Val d'Elsa, Tavarnelle Val di Pesa, San Casciano Val di Pesa, Impruneta, San Donato, Bagno a Ripoli, and back to Florence. It does not cover the area around Fiesole, north of the Arno, or the extreme eastern slices of the zone from Pelago to Reggello and from Rignano sull'Arno to Figline Valdarno. The whole route is about 120km (75 miles). Allow at least a couple of days.

Route: Florence

From Florence head onto the SS67, along the south bank of the Arno, past the urban sprawl, and under the A1 autostrada, to Lastra a Signa. This village's best-known estate, the 15th-century Villa Le Sorti (www.villalesorti.it), offers its tastefully restored chapel for weddings.

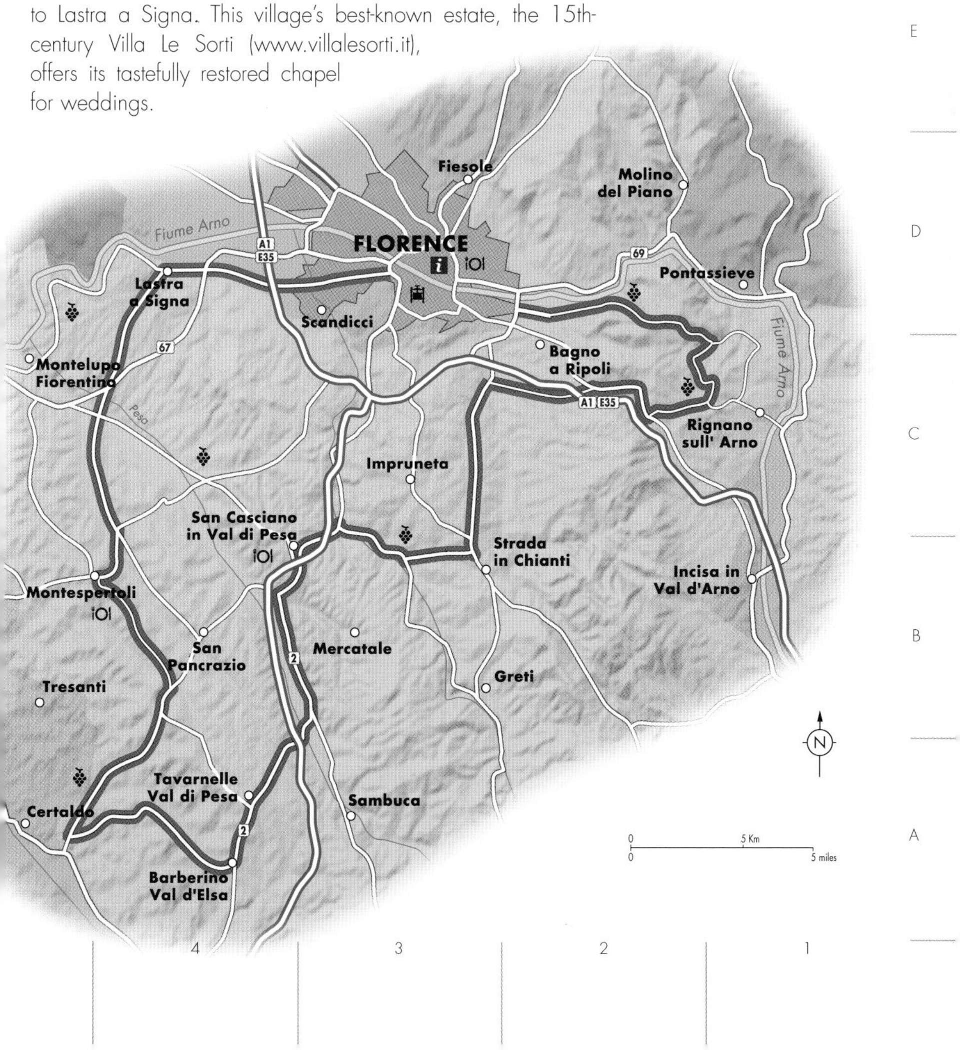

Route: Florence
Allow at least two days

Chianti Rùfina and Pomino

Florence (Chianti Colli Fiorentini) and Montespertoli

Chianti Classico

RIGHT *The Medici palace
guarded by a copy of
Michelangelo's David.*

BELOW *A glimpse of the
Duomo from a street corner.*

From the centre of Lastra a Signa take the road to Montespertoli, but turn right at San Romolo for the hamlet of Malmantile for Tenuta San Vito in Fior di Selva (*see* p.64). This is one of Tuscany's historic organic estates, and was converted to organics in 1982 by its owners, the Drighi family. Good quality, brick-coloured Chianti reds, crisp, oily dry whites from the Verdicchio grape, plus sparkling wine and *vin santo* are made. The estate also has its own olive oil press with a grindstone, which visitors are shown on guided tours. There is also a restaurant offering organic menus, plus three tranquil farmhouses with open fireplaces and a pool, for agritourism.

You can divert from here to Montelupo Fiorentino, crossing the Pesa River for Fattoria di Petrognano (tel: 0571 913795; www.petrognano.it), a large wine and olive oil estate with two restored 18th-century farmhouses for agritourism.

On to Montespertoli

Back on the Lastra a Signa–Montespertoli road turn right at the crossroads in Ginestra Fiorentina, then turn left towards Cerbaia for Fattoria San Michele a Torri (*see* p.64). Here, owner Paolo Nocentini produces a big range of wines from stone-arched cellars containing wooden vats and barrels mounted (unusually) on wooden plinths. Solid Chiantis, soft sparkling wines, and intense *vin santos* are made, all from organic grapes.

Head south for Montespertoli, which recently became a Chianti sub-zone. The leading estate, Fattoria Castello Sonnino (tel: 0571 609198; www.castellosonnino.it), dates from the 13th century and is also known as the Castle of Montespertoli (but it is not to be confused with Castello di Sonnino near Grosseto).

Owner Barone Alessandro de Renzis Sonnino is both a *bon vivant* and a big fan of Cabernet Sauvignon, whose blackcurrant influence can be felt in the estate's thick, chewy reds such as "Sanleone" and "Cantinio". The baron's wife, Caterina, designs wine labels for some of Tuscany's leading producers, including "Le Difese" and "Guidalberto" for Nicolò Incisa della Rocchetta of Sassicaia, "Suolo" for Tenuta di Argiano in Montalcino, and the Tenuta del Terriccio range (www.caterinaderenzis.it).

Other producers in Montespertoli include the architecturally impressive Castello di Poppiano (www.conteguicciardini.it) – whose Chianti Colli Fiorentini reds are atypically soft – and Podere

Biovino (tel: 0571 657185; podere.biovino@tele2.it), which, as its name suggests, is organic. Owner Lorenzo Rizzotti used to be an agronomist, then a farm manager, but became his own boss when he founded Podere Biovino in 1998. Rizzotti and his son Diego look to produce light Chiantis for early drinking (ideal picnic wines) and very aromatic olive oil.

Another organic Montespertoli domain is I Casciani (tel: 0571 608580). This is a classic mixed farm, with animals, arable crops, and red wines like the I Casciani Chianti, which exhibits the Sangiovese grape's classic bitter note, and the more internationally styled Villa Gaja red, in which Sangiovese's bitterness is softened by oak. The estate also makes its own vinegar in Modena, in Emilia-Romagna.

Also worth a detour is Maria and Carolina Alvino's Tenuta La Cipressaia (see p.69) whose Chianti Colli Fiorentini, made from Sangiovese with a bit of Colorino for colour, is well constructed. The Alvinos ferment some grapes as whole, not crushed, berries, which gives added softness.

A moment for contemplation

From Montespertoli head via Lucardo, where there is a fine view eastwards towards Certaldo, where the poet Boccaccio wrote *The Decameron*.

Just after Lucardo and on the way into Certaldo on the San Cascian–Certaldo road you'll find Ugo Bing's Fattoria di Fiano (www.fattoriadifiano.it), a source of crisp reds sculpted from limestone-dominated soils. Organic Certaldo producers

WHERE TO EAT

Gustavino [D3]
Via della Dondotta, 37
50121 Firenze (FI)
Tel: 055 2399806
info@gustavino.it
www.gustavino.it
Wine bar serving hot (pasta, tripe) and cold food (sandwiches, ham, sushi) with an inventive modern twist. Close to Piazza della Repubblica. Closed Monday. Sells wines from all over Italy as well.

Ristorante Casalta [B3]
Via Certaldese, 14/16
50026 San Casciano
Val di Pesa (FI)
Tel: 055 8248254
Clean, airy restaurant with wood-fired pizza oven, down-to-earth fish dishes, and children's menus. Moderately priced and fairly snappy service, though little atmosphere.

ABOVE *The stunning view of Florence from the Duomo.*

WINE SHOPS

Alimentari Pane & Co [D3]
Piazza S. Firenze, 5/R
50122 Firenze (FI)
Tel: 055 2654272
info@paneeco.it
www.paneeco.it
Former grocery, now
with a good selection
of Italian wines and
excellent, individual
cheeses, sausages,
hams, and mustards.

**Casa del Vino di Migliorini
Bruno e C. Snc [D3]**
Via dell'Ariento, 16/R
50100 Firenze (FI)
Tel: 055 215609
casadelvino@casadelvino.it
www.casadelvino.it
Centrally located wine
shop, popular with
tourists, with old-style
Tuscan furnishings.

here include Manfred Beiwinkel's Riparbello (which offers down-to-earth, good value agritourism, popular with Germans; *see* www.riparbello.it) and the more chaotic but charming Il Casale (*see* p.101).

The Gigoli family has farmed here since 1770, with the only interruption happening during the war when the house was destroyed by a stray bomb. Creamy but oak-free dry white wines and soft-centred reds are made, as well as fine olive oil and grappa, plus vinegar sold in a smoked glass bottle with a ribbon and a wax seal.

Industrial excursion

From Certaldo continue to Barberino Val d'Elsa for two rather industrial estates, Le Torri di Campiglioni (tel: 055 807616; campiglioni@tin.it) and Pasolini Dall'Onda Borghese (tel: 055 8075019; info@pasolinidallonda.com). Then from Barberino Val d'Elsa continue south if you want to go into Chianti Classico or turn northeast towards Tavarnelle Val di Pesa to stay within the Chianti Colli Fiorentini zone.

Between Barberino and Tavarnelle is Jan Karel Wäspi's Fattoria Villa Spoiano *see* box, right), a source of fairly priced and not-too-nutty *vin santo*, soft Merlot-based reds, and quaffable Chianti Colli Fiorentini.

The good, the bad, and the olive oil

Head north from Tavarnelle on the SS2, past Il Cantuccio

(www.ilcantuccio.net), which makes an inaccurately named red called "Excellente" and rather better olive oil, to San Casciano Val di Pesa. The historically renowned Fattoria di Lucignano is a 16th-century villa approached via a long, cypress-lined entrance with olive groves either side. It is being challenged quality-wise by the up-and-coming Castelvecchio (see box, right), whose most distinctive wine is the 100% Canaiolo red called "Numero Otto", aged in French barrels, and with a prune and vanilla flavour.

Enjoy the scenery

Even more assured reds come from the Goldschmitt family's Fattoria Corzano e Paterno (tel: 055 8248179; www.corzanoepaterno.it). They include the reliably modern Chianti Riserva "I Tre Borri". The wines from what is arguably San Casciano's prettiest vineyard, Fattoria Il Corno (tel: 055 824851; www.tenutailcorno.com), show sticky hedgerow fruit. This estate was established by an old Florentine family, Del Corno, in the 12th century. Today it covers 210 hectares, of which around 80 are used for vineyards while the others are planted to some 10,000 olive trees. The estate also makes a range of grappas.

Stay in the vineyards

From San Casciano head to Impruneta north on the SS2, then east via Il Ferrone for Il Termine (see p.64), which has three decent sized apartments for rental, a bed of crocuses for saffron production, and makes a well-balanced Chianti Colli Fiorentini with inspiring red fruit flavours, which opens out well within five years of harvest. Other Impruneta wineries include the (surprisingly) highly rated La Querce (tel: 055 2011380; www.laquerce.com), whose reds have varnishy aromas, and Fattoria di Bagnolo, whose winery shop sells grappa, olive oil, cherry marmalade, and olive paste.

From Impruneta take the SP222 north towards Florence, turning right just before the A1 motorway towards San Donata in Collina and Fattoria Torre a Cona (see p.64), said to be one of Tuscany's most striking 18th-century residences in the austere Florentine style. The wines mix sugar-sweet fruit with typically aggressive Sangiovese tannins.

Head north on windy roads via the hamlets of Castellonchio and Villamagna to Vallina on the edge of the Arno for Fattoria Le Sorgenti (see p.64; by appointment). The Ferrari family (who speak English) produce softly textured Chianti del Colli Fiorentini with appealing bitter cherry flavours, plus the more internationally styled and more blackcurrant-like Cabernet Sauvignon/Merlot blend called "Scirus". Follow the Arno west back to Florence.

Pisa

Pisa's leaning tower may be the most obvious attraction in this part of Tuscany for modern tourists, but since Roman times the area has been known for its thermal baths and hot springs, in towns like San Giuliano and San Casciano. Modern wine drinkers should now consider something other than spa towns, if coming here in search of something warm and wet, as the region's Chianti and other red wines have a warm prickle of alcohol to match their vibrant fruit.

ABOVE *The leaning tower, on every tourist's list.*

LOCAL INFORMATION

APT (Agenzia per il Turismo) di Pisa [D4]
Via Pietro Nenni, 24
56124 Pisa (PI)
Tel: 050 929777
aptpisa@pisa.turismo.toscana.it
www.pisa.turismo.toscana.it
Can handle general tourist and wine-specific enquiries.

Hidden treasures
The region's sandy soils give the red wines here their softness while the low-lying hills of the Arno River valley open up to the heat of the Mediterranean, providing the wines with their inner warmth. The region is a bit of a tourist backwater, with most visitors concentrating their fire on Pisa's leaning tower, the coast, or Etruscan towns like Volterra to the south.

The Pisa wine region is also often described as "emerging" but there is a case to say that it has already arrived, with several domains like Sangervasio, Ghizzano, and I Giusti e Zanza of top quality, emerging ones like Badia a Morrona, and one of Tuscany's best cooperatives too.

Don't write off Pisa's hills (le Colline Pisane) just because there are so few medieval castles and aristocratic villas compared to other Chianti zones like Colli Fiorentini or the Colli Senesi. Pisa's wine-growers are shaking off their association with Chianti anyway, by inventing a new designation for their Sangiovese-based reds called Terre di Pisa; and although the Pisan hills suit red wines better than dry whites, those sold under the Bianco di San Torpé designation tend to be well made, if inconsequential. The best growers, however, will get their vines to drag up some of the mineral richness present in these soils – usually iron, which makes for bricky- or leathery-tasting reds – into their wines for extra interest. And if it's real leather you're after, Pisa is famous in Italy for its leather goods. Contact the tourist office for details of the best shops, depending on whether bags, shoes, or accessories are your thing.

Getting there
Pisa is easily reached on the A1 (from Rome), A11 (from Florence), or A12 (from Genoa) motorways. Train services from Florence arrive at the main railway station on Piazza della Stazione. Near here on Piazza San Antonio you can catch local bus services operated by Lazzi (tel: 050 46288) and CPT (tel: 050 505511). Pisa also has an international airport.

Travelling around

Route summary The route forms a balloon shape from Pisa, via the towns and villages of Cenaia, Fauglia, Casciana Terme, Terricciola, Ghizzano, Palaia, and back to Pisa. The route is 100km (62 miles) long. Allow a couple of days to get the most out of this route.

Route: Pisa

Starting from Pisa take the SS206 south towards Cecina, turning left after 12km (8 miles) at Vicarello to reach Cenaia and Pisa's main wine cooperative, the Cantine delle Colline Pisane (*see* p.72). Wine quality here is surprisingly good, and in the fun shop on-site you can stock up on bag-in-box red and dry white wines for picnics. The wines in bottle proudly bear the cross of the Pisan Republic (La Repubblica Marinara di Pisa).

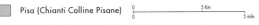

━━━━ Route: Pisa
      Allow two days

▨ Pisa (Chianti Colline Pisane)

0 ─────── 5 Km
0 ─────── 5 mile

WHERE TO EAT

L'Aeroscalo [C3]
Via Roma, 8
56025 Pontedera (PI)
Tel: 0587 52024
The "little airport". Eels and frogs' legs are specialities.

Quattro Gigli [C2]
Piazza Michele da Montopoli, 2
56020 Montopoli in Val d'Arno (PI)
Tel: 0571 466878/940
Attentive cooking with a terrace and comfortable accommodation, plus shop.

Ristorante La Greppia [B2]
Piazza del Carmine, 20/21
56037 Peccioli (PI)
Tel: 0587 672011
Big wine list and modern, Swiss-influenced cooking.

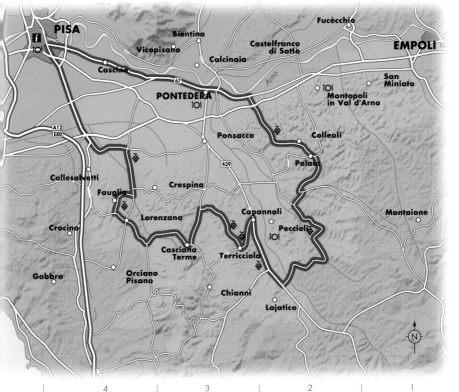

WINERIES IN PISA

PRICES: moderate

Badia di Morrona [B2]
Via di Badia, 8
56030 Terricciola (PI)
Tel: 0587 658505
info@badiadimorrona.it
www.badiadimorrona.it

Cantine delle Colline Pisane SCARL [C3]
Loc 4 Strade
Via Provinciale Livornese, 30
56040 Cenaia di Crespina (PI)
Tel: 050 643996
cantina@
cantinacollinepisane.it
www.cantinacollinepisane.it

I Giusti & Zanza [B4]
Via dei Puntoni, 9
56043 Fauglia (PI)
Tel: 0585 44354
info@igiustiezanza.it
www.igiustiezanza.it

Pieve de' Pitti [B2]
Via Pieve de' Pitti, 7
56030 Terricciola (PI)
Tel: 0587 635724
wine@pievedepitti.it
www.pievedepitti.it

Podere La Chiesa [B2]
Via di Casanova, 13
56030 Terricciola (PI)
Tel: 0587 653286
mamajero@libero.it

San Gervasio [C2]
Loc San Gervasio
56036 Palaia (PI)
Tel: 0587 483360 (office)
or 0587 629233 (winery)
info@sangervasio.com
www.sangervasio.com

Tenuta di Ghizzano [B2]
Via della Chiesa, 13
Fraz Ghizzano
56030 Peccioli (PI)
Tel: 0587 630096
info@tenutadighizzano.com
www.tenutadighizzano.com

Building a reputation

From Cenaia head towards Fauglia via Ceppaiano and Tripalle for 8km (5 miles) for one of the region's most innovative domains, I Giusti & Zanza (see box, left; by prior appointment). This was founded by schoolboy friends Paolo Giusti and Fabio Zanza (take Via Puntoni and keep going past the Locanda Giustiniani to the last house on the left).

Paolo is a construction engineer and says he "got into wine as a hobby, and now it takes 50 per cent of my time". He designed special fermentation tanks to be able to remove the pips from Sangiovese grapes during red winemaking, to prevent bitterness. The vineyards are planted at very high density (up to 10,000 vines per hectare) so each vine bears only a small number of grapes. I Giusti & Zanza's very concentrated reds include the exotic Sangiovese/Merlot "Belcore", the smoky, blackcurrant-flavoured Cabernet/Merlot "Dulcamara", and a bright-tasting Syrah. I Giusti & Zanza's experimental dry white wine from Trebbiano and Semillon is deliciously creamy (but unoaked).

Bird watching?

Also in Fauglia is the Fattoria Uccelliera (see box, right). The estate, amongst woodland on hills just outside the town, gets its name from the fact that birds used to be caught here in nets. The wines are rather simple, but each new vintage is labelled with a different bird.

From Fauglia it's a 24km (15 mile) journey to Terricciola via Lorenzana and the spa town of Casciana Terme. See the website, www.termedicasciana.it, for details of weekly or weekend spa treatments, gym facilities, and swimming pools.

Between Casciana Terme and Terricciola is the hamlet of Soiano where Ursula and Peter Mock's eponymously named estate lies (tel: 0587 654180; by appointment). They bought it recently from the Canadian couple Bruno and Elyane Moos, who acquired what was then called Castello di Soiano in 1983. Look out for reds called "Fontestina" and "Soianello".

Softly, softly

Keep going for the dynamic wine domain of Badia di Morrona (see box, left). The estate is a former abbey with 11th-century origins and now belongs to insurance specialists, the Gaslini family. The vineyards are on predominantly sandstone soil, which helps give the red wines a soft, docile character, making them appealing for drinking within a couple of years of the harvest. The Sangiovese, Cabernet, and Merlot red "N'Antia", which you'll find in a few local restaurants, is a good example, as is the Chianti "I Sodi del Paretaio". The top wine, "VignAalta", comes from the oldest Sangiovese vineyards and the oaked Chardonnay/Trebbiano "La Suvera" is fresh and well constructed.

Carry on into Terricciola and head towards the SP439 Capànnoli–Lajàtico road. On the way you'll pass Mario and Maité Bizzarri's Podere La Chiesa (*see* box, left; by prior appointment). There are just five hectares of vines, and only one red is made, Sabiniano du Casanova, from Sangiovese with 40% Cabernet Sauvignon and Merlot. Barrel-ageing is kept to a minimum, keeping the price of this refined wine tasting of soft, black fruit at an affordable level.

Turn right onto the SP49 towards Lajàtico and on the right after just over 1km (0.8 miles) you'll see the Gargari family's Pieve de' Pitti (*see* box, left). On the track up you'll pass a 500-year-old olive tree.

ABOVE *Vines dormant before bursting into life in spring.*

In 1972 the (English-speaking) Gargari family bought the estate, whose name means "the church of the Pitti family", after its late-17th-century owners (there is still a chapel here). Light wines are produced in an agreeably easy style like "Aprilante", an unoaked dry white blend of 60% Malvasia and 40% Vermentino, and the 100% Sangiovese red "Moro di Pava". Owner Sergio Gargari's architect daughter Caterina is an expert on environmentally friendly winery design.

Around Ghizzano

Before Lajàtico turn off the SS439 towards Ghizzano and the Tenuta di Ghizzano (*see* box, left; by appointment). Owners Pierfrancesco and Ginevra Venerosi Pesciolini's family arrived here in the 14th-century. Their domain produces intense, classy reds like the Merlot "Nambrot" and the Sangiovese, Cabernet, and Merlot "Veneroso", super *vin santo*, organic olive oil, and has beautifully atmospheric cellars.

From Ghizzano head via Montefoscoli to Palaia. About 8km (5 miles) past Palaia in the direction of Collèoli is Luca Tommasini's San Gervasio estate (*see* box, left). This offers agritourism, hunting opportunities, fanatically tended high density vineyards, and some of Tuscany's most impressive organic wines. The 100% Merlot "I Renai" and the Sangiovese-dominated "A Sirio" are great references for these tricky grapes, while the blended red "Sangervasio" is a benchmark Chianti Colline Pisane, being lightly floral and open-textured. Trebbiano-dominated *vin santo* is as big and serious as the burly Tommasini. Head back to Pisa via Pontedera on the SS67.

Siena

S iena is one of Tuscany's most admired cities – unless you are a Florentine, of course. In medieval times, as independent city-states Florence and Siena fought each other ceaselessly for political and financial reasons; Florence resented Siena taking all of its banking business. Even today, Florentine parents will raise their eyebrows an extra millimetre if their sons or daughters choose to marry a Sienese – and vice versa.

Vineyards as far as the eye can see

You don't have to drag yourself away from Siena's architectural gems to appreciate how significant the province is as a wine-producer. Climb the tower of the Palazzo Pubblico on Piazza del Campo (open daily with ticket; www.comune.siena.it) and you'll see Chianti Classico vineyards to the northeast, Montepulciano's and Montalcino's vineyards to the southeast and southwest respectively, with most of what's left falling under Siena's own Chianti designation of Colli Senesi. As there is generally less limestone and more clay in the soil here compared to Chianti Classico, Siena's Chiantis have plenty of colour and a noticeable bite. Some critics reckon that Chiantis from the Siena area are among Tuscany's most perfumed red wines; and after Chianti Classico this is the most important Chianti zone in terms of size.

Racing away

Try to avoid coming to the Siena area on July 2 and August 16 when a bareback horse race between the city's *contrade* (wards) called *Il Palio* takes place on Piazza del Campo. It's a great – if short (three minutes each time) – spectacle, although there are also warm-up races to see which of Siena's *contrade* will be competing on the day.

The race is hyped for all it's worth, and its renown means that places to both stay and eat in Siena get booked out months in advance. But if you are lucky enough to find somewhere to stay, you can watch the *Palio* for free if you stand in the Piazza del Campo – though you'll have to get there at the crack of dawn to beat the crowds. Tickets can be bought for the seated area, but they are expensive. Try Balzana Viaggi (tel: 0577 285013) or Siena Viaggi (tel: 0577 46484) in Siena for tickets.

However, if you fancy watching a race where it's horsepower rather than horses that makes a difference, the *Mille Miglia* ("thousand miles") is a grand prix rally for veteran cars. It crosses Siena province and stops in Piazza del Campo every May (*see* www.millemiglia.it).

Back to nature

To find some peace during the *Palio* and *Mille Miglia*, head off into the *crete senesi*, the lunar-like farmland south of Siena. Or get away from it all by booking a ride on the *Treno Natura* (Nature Train), which provides a stress-free way to explore the southern parts of Siena province like the Sienese Crete, the Val d'Orcia (covered in the chapter on Montepulciano), Monte Amiata, and the Ombrone Valley in a 140km (87 mile) circle that begins and ends in Siena. Some of the trains are steam-powered and, as there are three runs a day you can get off to explore if you take the morning train, miss the midday one, and get back on for the afternoon ride back to Siena (*see* www.ferrovieturistiche.it).

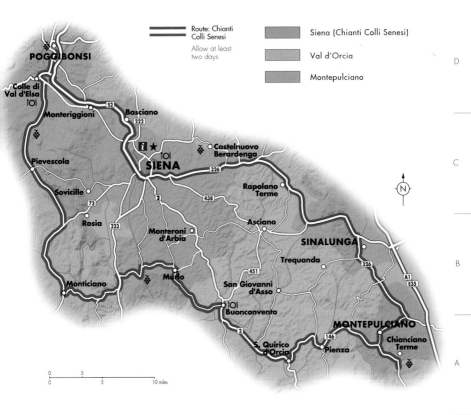

WHERE TO BUY WINE

Antica Drogheria
Manganelli, 1879
Via di Città 71/73
53100 Siena (SI)
Tel: 0577 280002
admanganelli@tin.it
Centrally located foodie
paradise offering a wide
range of top-quality foods.
The location and reputation
mean bargains are rare.

La Bottega di Casanova
Castelsangimignano, 27
53030 San Gimignano (SI)
Tel: 0577 953202
Organic sun-dried tomatoes,
olive oil, marmalade,
sauces, honey, Chianti Colli
Senesi, and Vernaccia. Free
tastings.

Cantina in Piazza
Via Casato di Sotto, 24
53100 Siena (SI)
Tel: 0577 222758
www.cantinainpiazza.it
Holds wine tastings in
English if you book ahead.

Consorzio Agrario Siena
Via Pianigiani, 9
53100 Siena (SI)
Tel: 0577 222368
www.capsi.it
Supermarket selling food
and wine from the farmers'
consortium (Consorzio
Agrario). Similar shops
in Buonconvento, Pienza,
Chianciano Terme, and
Montalcino. Closed Sunday.

Enoteca Italiana
Fortezza Medicea, 1
53100 Siena (SI)
Tel: 0577 288487
Huge wine shop in vaulted
cellars under Medicean
fortress. Closed Sunday.

Enoteca San Domenico
Via del Paradiso, 56
53100 Siena (SI)
Tel: 0577 271181
Well-chosen selection

Getting there

Siena can be reached easily by train and regular services run
from Florence's main railway station, Santa Maria Novella.
SITA bus services also operate from Florence: it takes around
90 minutes to reach Siena. SENA bus services travel from
Rome or Perugia. If you are travelling by car from the north,
take the Certosa exit off the A1 motorway at Florence and
follow the "4 corsie" (dual carriageway) to Siena.

Travelling around

Route summary From Siena drive east to Castelnuovo
Berardenga, then travel south via Montepulciano to
Chianciano Terme. From here you can then go back via
Buonconvento and Murlo towards Siena to see the northern
part of the zone around Colle di Val d'Elsa, before heading
back to Siena. The total route length is around 250 km (156
miles), so allow at least a couple of days.

Route: Chianti Colli Senesi

From Siena take the main road east in the direction of
Arezzo, turning left after 20km (12.5 miles) for Castelnuovo
Berardenga, a *comune* located on the edge of the
Chianti Colli Senesi and Chianti Classico border. One of
the biggest estates here, Fattoria Chigi Saracini (tel: 0577
355113), is owned by the Sienese banking group Monte

dei Paschi di Siena. The estate is large, covering a total of 900 hectares, of which around 60 hectares are given over to vines. Recommended wines produced at Fattoria Chigi Saracini include a fairly exuberant Chianti Colli Senesi called "Bergallo" and an IGT red named "Il Poggiassi", a blend which is lightened by a high percentage of fruit from young vines.

More textured reds are made in Castelnuovo Berardenga by Stefano Borsa and his family at Pacina (see box on p.78). Both the hamlet of Pacina and this domain centre on what was once a 10th-century convent. Pacina is a mixed farm, with woodland, olives, cereals, and forage for farm animals, plus fruit and vegetables, as well as vines. The family has farmed here for five generations and makes Sangiovese-based reds with simple but bright fruit.

From Pacina it's quite a long drive of 45km (28 miles) to reach the next winery on our route, as we have to travel through the eastern edge of the Val d'Orcia (Orcia Valley) and Montepulciano to reach the spa town of Chianciano Terme. Drive via Rapolano Terme, Sinalunga, Torrita di Siena (which is named after its medieval look-out tower), and Montepulciano.

Let it grow

Sensi Terra d'Arcoiris (see p.78) lies on the Chiusi road from Chianciano Terme on the left before the Esso garage. Owners Paola Leonardi and Walter Loesch have left the soil in the vineyard untouched for the last 20 years, adding no compost as fertilizer and not ploughing weeds away – a practice which is highly unusual and goes against "modern" farming methods.

"I let the grass grow, like my hair," says Walter, a one-time philosophy scholar. In this way the topsoils have found their natural balance as native grasses have squeezed out the noxious weeds and the vine roots have had to dig deeper for food and water with so much competing vegetation. You can tell the vines are especially deep rooting by the taste of the Terra d'Arcoiris Colli Senesi reds – and the estate's grape

LEFT *There is a wealth of food shops and delicatessens.*

BELOW *Insignia depicting family crests or trades can be seen on buildings.*

WINERIES IN CHIANTI COLLI SENESI

PRICES: moderate

Cantina Sociale Vini Senesi e Fiorentini [D4]
Loc Fontana, 23
Staggia Senesi
53036 Poggibonsi (SI)
Tel: 0577 930886
chiantiwines@inwind.it

Casale (Borella) [C4]
Casale Collato, 3
53034 Colle di Val d'Elsa (SI)
Tel: 0577 929718
casalewines@temainf.it
www.casalewines.com

Fattoria Casabianca [B3]
Fraz Casciano di Murlo
Loc Monte Pescini
53016 Murlo (SI)
Tel: 0577 811033
infoagriturismo@
fattoriacasabianca.it
www.fattoriacasabianca.it

Pacina [C3]
Loc Pacina
53019 Castelnuovo
Berardenga (SI)
Tel: 0577 355044
pacinina@libero.it
www.pacina.it

Terra d'Arcoiris [A1]
Strada della Maglianella, 5
53042 Chianciano Terme (SI)
Tel: 0578 60270
terradarcoiris@libero.it
www.terradarcoiris.it

juice, which is sold by the litre. The wines are incredibly concentrated and mouth-filling, tasting of minerals previously locked deep underground. As well as the wines you will find peach, prune, pear, and quince jams and olive oil for sale, too. There are also rooms and flats for rental (*see* the website for details).

French favourites

South of Chianciano Terme in the village of Sarteano you will find the brilliant Andrea Franchetti's Tenuta di Trinoro (tel: 0578 267110; www.tenutaditrinoro.it). Franchetti favoured the Bordeaux grapes such as Cabernets Franc and Sauvignon, Merlot, and Petit Verdot over Sangiovese when he planted his deserted hillside site from 1991. Low yields, winemaking by hand, and careful oak-ageing make for concentrated wines that both the critics and consumers adore – hence you can't buy the wines direct and visits are strictly by prior appointment.

Around Murlo

From Chianciano Terme head towards Buonconvento via Montepulciano and San Quirico d'Orcia. Travelling on from Buonconvento follow the signs to Bibbiano, then Murlo. If you have time to stop here, an up-and-coming small producer in Murlo, in the hamlet of Montepescini (due south of Casabianca), is the genial Massimiliano Governi's Fattoria Montepescini (tel: 0577 817876; www.fattoriamontepescini.it). Governi makes crisp red wines from vineyards surrounding this thousand-year-old hamlet.

RIGHT *Barrels waiting for refurbishment or recycling.*

More than just wine

Continuing on from Murlo follow the signs to Casciano di Murlo for Fattoria Casabianca (see box, left). The total distance from Chianciano Terme is 60km (38 miles). This huge estate produces red and pink wines in a value-for-money, easy-drinking style, but also offers a wide range of agritourism opportunities including apartments to rent and activities such as swimming, tennis, horse-riding, fishing, cycling, and hiking.

Organic opportunities

To continue the route get onto the Siena–Grosseto road, travelling in the direction of Grosseto (south) and almost immediately turn right to Monticiano, taking the road north along the Elsa River towards Colle di Valle d'Elsa. Stop after 50km (30 miles) at Collalto for Giovanni Borella's Casale estate (see box, left). Vibrant sparkling whites, satisfying pink wines, and classy Chianti Colli Senesi are produced from hilly vineyards overlooking the Elsa River valley. As well as the wines you can try some of the estate's thick honey. There are also camping facilities here and you can pitch your tent around an old oak tree with a natural fountain, in an idyllic setting amongst Borella's organic olive groves and vines. English is spoken.

Another organic producer worth watching in Colle di Val d'Elsa is La Colombaia (tel: 0577 971081) managed by Nadia Castagnedi and her son Dante. Like Borella, they arrived here in the 1970s, but have started to bottle wine from their own grapes only in the last couple of years.

Clear as crystal

Colle di Val d'Elsa is also well known for the manufacture of crystal and glass. Visit the Museo del Cristallo (Via dei Fossi, 8A, 53034 Colle Val d'Elsa; tel: 0577 924135; www.cristallo.org) to see how crystal is made, and there is a sound and light show too, where you can hear the harmonious effect air movement has on crystal.

From Colle di Val d'Elsa keep going north for 16km (10 miles) towards Poggibonsi, which is one of Tuscany's ugliest towns. It was heavily bombed during World War II, being a strategic railway junction, and the prefabricated feel of the Cantina Sociale Vini Senesi e Fiorentini (see box, left) is entirely in keeping with the rest of the town architecturally. All the same, this is not a bad place to stock up on cheap wine boxes and bottles for picnics.

To finish the route, from Poggibonsi simply head back to Siena on the Siena–Florence dual carriageway. The journey is 24km (15 miles).

WHERE TO EAT

Enoteca "I Terzi" [C4]
Via dei Termini, 7
53100 Siena (SI)
Tel: 0577 44329
Smart but not pretentious, with excellent wine and good service. Try fresh green or bean salads or ricotta pasta to start; duck and rabbit in rich sauces for second course; and panna cotta for dessert. Closed Sunday.

Locanda Arnolfo Ristorante [D4]
Via XX Settembre, 50/52a
53034 Colle Val d'Elsa (SI)
Tel: 0577 920549
Classy sheep's cheese ravioli, Sienese pork sauce, and pigeon roasted in vin santo with nuts and figs. Closed Tuesday.

Nonno Mede [C4]
Camporegio, 21
53100 Siena (SI)
Tel: 0577 247966
Reasonably priced pizzeria with huge choice but consistent quality. Closed Tuesday.

Osteria Nonna Gina [C4]
Via Pian dei Montellini
53100 Siena (SI)
Tel: 0577 287247
Small, family-run establishment popular with locals. Book ahead for subtle risotto and pasta and simple red wines.

Ristorante da Mario [A3]
Via Soccini, 60
53022 Buonconvento (SI)
Tel: 0577 806157
Friendly and simple family-run eatery in Buonconvento's main street offering hearty no-frills bean soups, simple salads, and tender grilled meats. Closed Saturday.

Arezzo

Arezzo generally gets a pretty bad press. The province is home to Chianti Colli Aretini, or the "Chianti from the Arezzo hills". This red wine is invariably described as light, soft, and not too structured; but to most modern wine drinkers looking for a simple glass of red these are positive virtues. Arezzo has never had much renown as a wine-producer – the soils are seen as too light and the climate too hot and humid for the finest wines – and, historically, tobacco thrived here. The local Chianina cattle also do very well on the sweet grass. One advantage of all this is that Arezzo's wines have always offered good value.

LOCAL INFORMATION

Agenzia per il Turismo di Arezzo [B2]
Piazza Risorgimento, 116
52100 Arezzo (AR)
Tel: 0575 23952
apt@arezzo.turismo.toscana.it
www.apt.arezzo.it

Uffici informazioni [B2]
Piazza della Repubblica, 28
52100 Arezzo (AR)
Tel: 0575 377678
info@arezzo.turismo.toscana.it

Both of the above can provide maps for the Strada del Vino and details of local wine festivals and Arezzo's antique market.

Not to be taken lightly

Make no mistake, there are some serious wines to be had here, especially away from the valley floor and on the slopes. Arezzo in fact has three valleys: the mountainous Casentino, in whose hills the Arno rises; the Arno itself; and the Val di Chiana, whose beef cattle are arguably the most renowned in Tuscany.

Crossing the plain, upon which the city of Arezzo sits, from one side of the Chiana canal to the other can be tiresome by car, such is the maze of light industrial estates, lugubriously slow traffic lights, and hazardous signposting.

Spend your time more profitably in the Protomagno and Casentino mountains east of Arezzo if you want some seclusion (there are two monasteries here), or west of the Chianti mountains (Monti del Chianti) overlooking the Arno between Montevarchi and Monte San Savino for deeper, more textured wines than the Aretini norm (Chianti Classico, let it be noted, is just over the ridge).

One irony, for a region seen as unable to produce wines lasting into antiquity, is Arezzo's antique market. This is said to be the oldest and largest antiques fair in Tuscany, founded in 1968 and with around 500 exhibitors from all over Italy. It takes place on the first Sunday of every month and the Saturday before (i.e. Saturday May 31 and Sunday June 1). See www.comune.arezzo.it for details.

Getting there

Travelling by car, Arezzo is a 12km (8 mile) drive east from the Rome–Florence A1 autostrada. The city is around 80km (50 miles) south of Florence and 210km (130 miles) from Rome. Arezzo is on the Florence–Rome main railway line. The town's

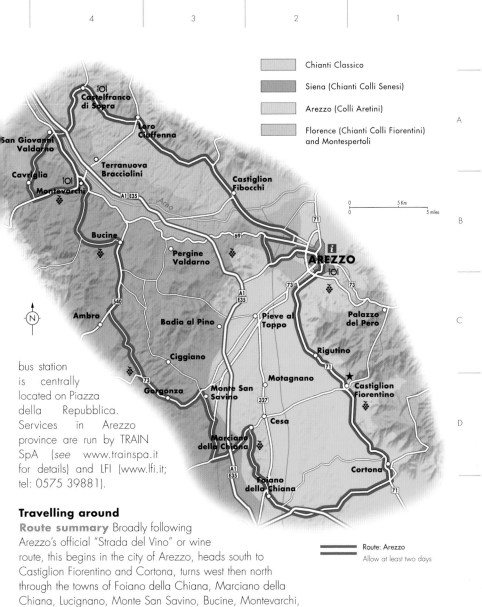

Chianti Classico

Siena (Chianti Colli Senesi)

Arezzo (Colli Aretini)

Florence (Chianti Colli Fiorentini)
and Montespertoli

Castelfranco
di Sopra

Loro
Ciuffenna

San Giovanni
Valdarno

Cavriglia

Terranuova
Bracciolini

Castiglion
Fibocchi

Montevarchi

Bucine

Pergine
Valdarno

AREZZO

Ambra

Badia al Pino

Pieve al
Toppo

Palazzo
del Pero

Ciggiano

Rigutino

bus station
is centrally
located on Piazza
della Repubblica.
Services in Arezzo
province are run by TRAIN
SpA (see www.trainspa.it
for details) and LFI (www.lfi.it;
tel: 0575 39881).

Gorgonza

Monte San
Savino

Motagnano

Castiglion
Fiorentino

Cesa

Marciano
della Chiana

Cortona

Foiano
della Chiana

Travelling around

Route summary Broadly following
Arezzo's official "Strada del Vino" or wine
route, this begins in the city of Arezzo, heads south to
Castiglion Fiorentino and Cortona, turns west then north
through the towns of Foiano della Chiana, Marciano della
Chiana, Lucignano, Monte San Savino, Bucine, Montevarchi,
San Giovanni, and Valdarno as far as Castelfranco di Sopra,
then heads southeast towards Arezzo via Loro Ciuffenna and
Castiglion Fibocchi. This covers 200km (125 miles). Allow at
least a couple of days.

Route: Arezzo
Allow at least two days

Route: Arezzo

From the centre of Arezzo you can easily head east towards
San Fabiano to visit Conti Borghini Baldovinetti de'Bacci's
beautiful house but unremarkable winery, the Fattoria San

WHERE TO EAT

Antica Osteria L'Agania [B2] Via Massini, 10 52100 Arezzo (AR) Tel: 0575 25381 Closed Monday. Soups, rabbit served as rare as you dare, and tripe.

Locanda al Castello di Sorci Via San Lorenzo, 21 Sorci 52031 Anghiari (AR) Tel: 0575 789066 Closed Monday. Tuscan classics like Chianina beef.

Osteria di Rendola [B4] Via di Rendola, Rendola, 52025 Montevarchi (AR) Tel: 0575 9707491 Closed Wednesday. Good value Tuscan staples.

Il Vicolo del Contento [A4] Mandri, 18 52020 Castelfranco di Sopra (AR) Tel: 055 9149277 Book ahead. Eclectic wine list and fish menu.

Fabiano (www.fattoriasanfabiano.it). The count's library – a 12th-century tower – contains original papers showing how his ancestors commissioned the most famous work of renowned fresco painter Piero della Francesca (c.1416–92), called *The Legend of the True Cross*. To see it, visit the church of San Francesco in Arezzo (by prior appointment; www.pierodellafrancesca.it).

From art to wine

For wine purposes head into Arezzo's southern suburbs for Villa Cilnia (*see* box, right). Take the SS73, direction Sansepolcro, turning right soon after Staggiano San Fiore towards the hamlet of Bagnoro where Villa Cilnia is located, along an avenue of cherry trees. The villa overlooks the Bagnoro Valley and dates from the 14th century. Owner Raffaele Galucci lets his brother-in-law, the hang-dog Luigi Segala run the 20 hectares of vineyards and olive groves. Luigi's partner Orietta Gustand looks after the holiday apartments, offering breakfast, a swimming pool, and barbecue facilities. There is also a small lake for those wishing to indulge in sport-fishing. The red wines here, like the oak-aged "Vocato" (Sangiovese with 20% Cabernet Sauvignon) and "Cign'Oro" (50% Sangiovese, 25% Cabernet Sauvignon, and 25% Merlot) are consistently appealing for their chocolate tones, with the Sangiovese-dominated "Ross'Oro" offering the easiest and best value drinking of all.

From Villa Cilnia head back towards Arezzo to get on the SS71 to Cortona, stopping after less than 8km (5 miles) in Castiglion Fiorentino for La Pievuccia (*see* boxes, right and p.84). The villa dates from the early 1800s, and has been owned by the Papini family since the 1930s. As well as wine, vegetables, grains, and olives, *cinta senesi* pigs, chickens, geese, and rabbits are produced. All are certified organic and are served in the winery's restaurant. Dip the bread, baked on site, into *acqua cotta*, a tasty soup served with an egg on the top. The red wines are simple quaffers with nice, wild, old-vine fruit.

From Castiglion Fiorentino head south to Cortona (*see* Montepulciano chapter), then turn right to Foiano della Chiana and Marciano della Chiana, crossing the low point of the Chiana Valley and the Chiana canal.

Just before Marciano and on the right-hand side is the Niccolai family's Fattoria Santa Vittoria (*see* boxes, right and p.84). The house was built in 1572 by Cosimo I dei Medici to commemorate the victory of the republic of Florence over Siena in the battle of Cannagallo. This is a mixed farm with 60 hectares of maize, olives, and sunflowers, and around 30 hectares of vineyards. An experimental vineyard contains 30 red and white Italian grape varieties which the owners are trying to resurrect; and there are also plantings of southern Italian grapes like Nero d'Avola for the black fruit-scented red wine "Poggio Grasso". Earthy *vin santo*, like chunky orange marmalade, the estate's Sangiovese-based reds like "Scannagallo" (with Cabernet Sauvignon) and "Poggio del Tempio" (with Merlot) are reliable and juicy, while the crisp, dry Grechetto-based whites offer good value.

Dizzying heights

From Santa Vittoria head west to the nearby village of Lucignano, then north to Monte San Savino. Here you join the SS73 west towards Castelnuovo Berardenga (*see* Chianti Classico chapter) but stop as the road reaches its highest point in the evergreen forests, 4km (2.5 miles) past Palazzuolo, for the organic Giacomo Marengo. You'll have to negotiate the chickens, turkeys, and peacocks running loose in the car park to find the tasting room and shop. Marengo's wines, such as Sangiovese-based Chianti reds, are made in an easy to approach style, while white wines like "Cuvée Sant'Anna" made from French varieties like Chardonnay and Sauvignon Blanc are not drowned by oak. There are three holiday apartments with original features, plus a swimming pool.

Follow the SS540 to Bucine, turning left when you get there to reach Fattoria Petrolo (*see* box, right). This ancient, rambling estate with Etruscan origins and discreet agritourism accommodation lies above the hamlet of Galatrona, which

WINERIES IN AREZZO
. . . .

Fattoria di Gratena [C2]
Loc Pieve a Maiano
52100 Arezzo (AR)
Tel: 0575 368664
gratena@katamail.com
www.gratena.it

Fattoria Petrolo [B4]
Loc Galatrona, 30
Fraz Mercatale Valdarno
52020 Montevarchi (AR)
Tel: 055 9911322
petrolo@petrolo.it
www.petrolo.it

Fattoria Santa Vittoria [D2]
Loc Pozzo, Via Piana, 43
52045 Foiano
della Chiana (AR)
Tel: 0575 66807
contact@fattoriasantavittoria.com

Giacomo Marengo [C4]
Fraz Capraia
Loc Palazzuolo
52048 Monte San Savino (AR)
Tel: 0575 847083
marengoe@tin.it
www.marengo.it

La Pievuccia [D1]
Via Santa Lucia, 118
52043 Castiglion
Fiorentino (AR)
Tel: 0575 651007
info@lapievuccia.it
www.lapievuccia.it

I Selvatici [B4]
Via Ricasoli, 61
52025 Montevarchi (AR)
Tel: 055 901146
info@iselvatici.it
www.iselvatici.it

Villa Cilnia [C2]
Loc Montoncello, 27
Fraz Bagnoro
52040 Arezzo (AR)
Tel: 0575 365017
villacilnia@interfree.it
www.villacilnia.com

LEFT *Driveway to Tenuta Il Borro, one of Italy's most modern wineries.*

Fattoria Santa Vittoria
[D2] Loc Pozzo
Via Piana, 43
52045 Foiano della
Chiana (AR)
Tel: 0575 660430
contact@
fattoriasantavittoria.com
www.fattoria
santavittoria.com
Four independent and
tasteful apartments in
a farm building located
in an isolated part of
the estate, with views
of the rolling Chiana
Valley. English spoken.

La Pievuccia [D1]
Via Santa Lucia, 118
52043 Castiglion
Fiorentino (AR)
Tel: 0575 651007
info@lapievuccia.it
www.lapievuccia.it
English and German
spoken. Self-contained
apartments, one called
"Mimosa" with wheelchair
access, plus swimming
pool (May–September),
mountain bike hire,
and courses in cookery
and silk painting.
Farm animals make this
child-friendly, too.

Residenza Loro [A4]
Via della Corte, 3
52024 Loro
Ciuffenna (AR)
Tel: 055 9166456
or 349 8451452
m.shah@tin.it
www.farmhouse-
tuscany.co.uk
Second floor apartment
in a 14th-century palazzo
with its own entrance
from the courtyard, good
views over the main
piazza, spacious, well-lit
rooms with frescoed
ceilings. The owner can
arrange winery visits,
too. English spoken.

gives its name to Petrolo's most famous red wine, a 100% Merlot made by the Sanjust family in an oaky, blockbuster style. The remains of a look-out tower lend its name to "Torrione", a pure Sangiovese red, aged in French oak barrels with unusual chocolate tannins and wiry acidity.

Continue towards Montevarchi where you drop down into the Arno Valley, and there turn left for I Selvatici, which is signposted (see boxes, right and p.83). The ebullient Sala family makes cleverly weighted Chianti Aretini reds and the 100% Sangiovese "Cardisco" and the only place you can buy them is in the winery shop (worldwide shipping available) – the rest is exported to the USA (winemaker Giuseppe Sala spent two years at Opus One in California). An appealing oxidized style of *vin santo* is also produced.

Fashion conscious
From Montevarchi, cross the Arno at San Giovanni Valdarno to reach Castelfranco di Sopra to begin the journey back to Arezzo. Two-thirds of the way between Loro Ciuffenna and Castiglion Fibocchi at San Giustino Valdarno is Tenuta Il Borro (www.ilborro.it), owned by the fashion-design Ferragamo family (see also Brunello di

Montalcino chapter). The huge, impressive winery lies close to the hamlet of Il Borro, which (apart from a bit of Church land) the Ferragamos also own. As well as providing accommodation for the vineyard workers, Il Borro has a very good restaurant, plus luxury and more down-to-earth houses and apartments for agritourism, as well as shops selling local crafts. Guests can also go hunting on the estate. Il Borro's red wines like "Pian di Nova" (Syrah and Sangiovese), "Polissena" (Sangiovese), and "Il Borro" (Merlot, Cabernet, Syrah, and Petit Verdot) show distinctive, almost sweet fruit.

Just south of Castiglion Fibocchi you'll find Tenuta Sette Ponti (tel: 055

977443; by prior appointment only), home of concentrated reds. The estate takes its name from the Ponte Buriano (built 1240–77) which you cross on your way to Arezzo. It features in the backdrop to Leonardo da Vinci's *Mona Lisa* and is one of the seven bridges crossing the Arno on the road from Arezzo to Florence.

A unique grape

Head back to Arezzo via Indicatore to pick up the SS69 road west (direction Al Autostrada) for the hamlet of Pieve a Maiano, just south of which is Fattoria di Gratena (*see* p.83). The estate has fantastic views over wooded hills, and a red grape variety, possibly unique to the estate, christened Gratena. Cuttings of this were sent to Milan University and compared to French and Italian vines with no genetic match being made. The Fattoria's Chiantis show concentrated, elegant old vine fruit and a crisp structure as the vineyards are relatively high (300 metres /984 feet). A bottling from the Gratena grape called "Siro" (with a bit of Syrah) shows almost exotic wild red fruit. There are peaceful holiday apartments. Only the bees, whose hives are placed in the woods for Gratena's honey, will disturb you.

LEFT *Red wines gently ageing in the quiet confines of a cellar.*

WHERE TO STAY

Il Pino Bioagricoltura [A4]
Via Castiglion Ubertini, 78
52028 Terranuova
Bracciolini (AR)
Tel: 055 9703807
mail@ilpino.com
www.ilpino.com
Eight independent apartments plus swimming pool in a soft, rural setting. Estate-grown organic produce such as dog rose honey, grape jam, and sweet Malvasia white wines available in the winery shop.

I Selvatici [B4]
Via Ricasoli, 61
52025 Montevarchi (AR)
Tel: 055 901146
info@iselvatici.it
www.iselvatici.it
Smart, characterful villa divided into three apartments plus swimming pool (small one). Tuscan specialities served in the winery's small dining area by prior booking. English spoken.

Tuscany Restored [C2]
Il Pero
Loc Manziana 15/16
52040 Rigutino (AR)
Tel: 0575 979593
info@ilpero.com
www.ilpero.com
English-owned villa offering its own and other local holiday homes for rental (and purchase). Featured in Channel Four's *No Going Back* TV programme in 2003.

Lucca, Carmignano, and northwest Tuscany

Don't listen to the world weary who say that northwest Tuscany's only function is to be the place one must cross to get to the "heart" of Tuscany, meaning Florence, Siena, and presumably points south. Tell that to Michelangelo, who made pilgrimages to Carra and its quarries of unique white marble, without which his *David* would not exist. The mainly white wine vineyards here, ideally containing Vermentino and Malvasia ("Candia") rather than Trebbiano, belong to the Colli dei Luni and the Colli Apuani, source of potentially blisteringly fresh whites.

Life on the edge

These are Tuscany's most spectacular, precipitously terraced vines, planted by hand and at absurdly high density, each vine hanging over the Mediterranean while clinging to a single post, like weary sailors to the mast in a thickening swell.

Further inland at Lucca and Montecarlo the terraces are wider, as olive trees and mainly red wine vines like Sangiovese, Syrah, and Merlot fight for space, producing red wines of glistening red and black fruit. The terraces are supported by dry stone walls peppered with wild flowers and shrubs.

Little channels dug by the side of the road offer you a place to dip your hands and cool your face as you stare west across to the shimmering heat of the Mediterranean, but they can prove fatal to your car's suspension and wheel arches – so look before you pull over to that perfect spot for a mountain picnic.

Further east at Carmignano vines and olives are overshadowed by Medici hunting villas, built when this area was the playground of Florence's masters. Wine tastings here are often accompanied by a plate of dried local figs, walnuts, or almond biscuits, for which Carmignano is famous. Track down the Amari twins, sisters Mariella and Lorella, of Biscotti M&L Amari (tel: 055 8711538) for fig cookies, fig vinegar, and conserves. The light "Barco Reale" and more structured "Carmignano" reds eloquently blend Italy's Sangiovese with Cabernet and Merlot – first brought here from France after Duke Cosimo III sought vinestocks for his vineyards after issuing his 1716 edict delimiting Carmignano's production zone.

Getting there

For Colli Apuani and Colli dei Luni, the Genoa–Rome line stops at Marina di Carrara. Buses are run by CAT (tel: 0585 85311). By car, exit the Genoa–Pisa A12 motorway at Massa.

For Lucca and Montecarlo exit the A11 Pisa–Viareggio motorway at Montepaschio. Buses are run by CLAP (tel: 0583 587897). Both cities are on the Florence–Viareggio railway.

Carmignano is best reached by road, taking the Prato–Calenzano exit from the A1 motorway, then following signs to Indicatore-Poggio a Caiano, or take either the Prato Ovest (west) or Prato Est (east) exit off the A11 and follow signs to Poggio a Caiano and Seano.

Travelling around

Route summaries There are three possible itineraries for this region of Tuscany.

Route One summary From the Marina di Carrara to Pontremoli, to Fosdinovo and Massa, and back to Marina di Carrara. Route length is approximately 75km (46 miles). Allow two days.

Route Two summary From Lucca to Monte San Quirico, Ponte a Moriano, Matraia, and Montecarlo. Route length is approximately 46km (29 miles). Allow two days.

Route Three summary From Carmignano to Comeana, Artimino, Bacchereto, Capezzana, and back to Carmignano. Route length is approximately 21km (13 miles). Allow one or two days.

Route One: Colli Apuani and Colli dei Luni

From the Marina di Carrara join the E80 motorway (direction Genova), taking the E31/A15 motorway (direction Parma) at the San Stefano La Spezia junction. Exit the A15 at the old town of Pontremoli. The town is overlooked from the west by the winery of Podere Benelli (www.poderebenelli.it), where traditional red grapes like Pollera and Merlarola are used with the Ciliegiolo to produce characterful, bitter reds whose taste is marked by rather old-style wood.

Equally traditional-style reds are made on the eastern edge of Pontremoli town by Fattoria Ruschi Noceti (see p.91) from local grapes like Pollera, Monfra, Marinello, and Morone. Stony clay soil gives wines of deepish colour and powerful tannins, and old wood flavours are fairly subdued.

From Pontremoli head south on the SP62 to the town of Aulla, where you take the SP63 to Rometta, then turn right onto the SP446 to Fosdinovo and Podere Lavandaro (see p.91). The car park is just a 200m (656 feet) walk from the modern winery producing dry Colli dei Luni Vermentino whites full of bitter almond and lime-peel flavours.

Another excellent source of Colli dei Luni Vermentino in Fosdinovo is Terenzuola (see p.91). The relatively young vines here give dry whites with plenty of zip, but soft pressing stops the fruit from tasting too bitter.

ABOVE *Fattoria Artimino's roof is covered with chimneys.*

WHERE TO EAT

Caveau del Teatro [F2]
Via del Teatro, 4
54027 Pontremoli (MS)
Tel: 0187 833328

Enoteca Ristorante Mamo Di Mariano Antoni [A5]
Via Chiesa, 63
55012 Gragnano (LU)
Tel: 0583 974079

La Nuova Iera [F2]
Loc Iera, 19
54021 Bagnone (MS)
Tel: 0187 428161

Ristorante Alle Vigne [C3]
Via dell'Uva, 5
54100 Massa (MS)
Tel: 0585 832540

Ristorante Mecenate [A5]
Via della Chiesa, 707
55050 Gattaiola (LU)
Tel: 0583 512167

Ristorante La Mora [A5]
Via Ludovica, 1748
55100 Sesto Di Moriano (LU)
Tel: 0583 406402

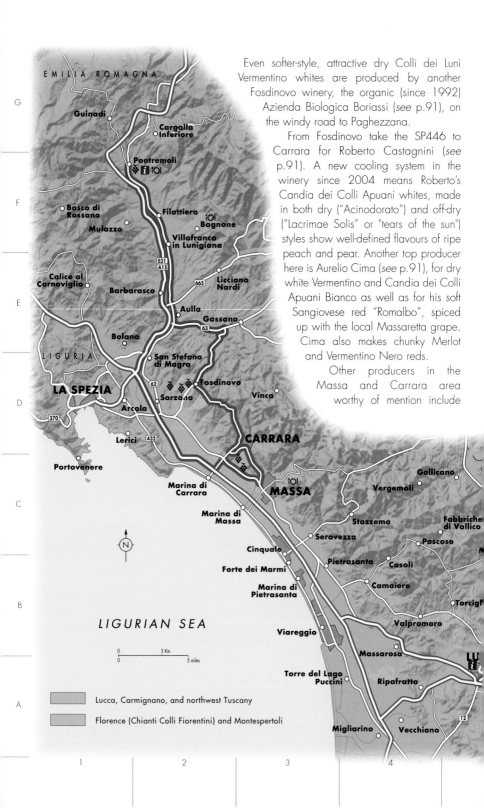

Even softer-style, attractive dry Colli dei Luni Vermentino whites are produced by another Fosdinovo winery, the organic (since 1992) Azienda Biologica Boriassi (see p.91), on the windy road to Paghezzana.

From Fosdinovo take the SP446 to Carrara for Roberto Castagnini (see p.91). A new cooling system in the winery since 2004 means Roberto's Candia dei Colli Apuani whites, made in both dry ("Acinodorato") and off-dry ("Lacrimae Solis" or "tears of the sun") styles show well-defined flavours of ripe peach and pear. Another top producer here is Aurelio Cima (see p.91), for dry white Vermentino and Candia dei Colli Apuani Bianco as well as for his soft Sangiovese red "Romalbo", spiced up with the local Massaretta grape. Cima also makes chunky Merlot and Vermentino Nero reds.

Other producers in the Massa and Carrara area worthy of mention include

Lucca, Carmignano, and northwest Tuscany

Florence (Chianti Colli Fiorentini) and Montespertoli

Podere Scurtarola (www.scurtarola.com), where PierPaolo Lorieri's appealing red and white wines are sold in the estate's delightful shop; Vin.Ca at Carrara-Avenza (tel: 0585 834217) for crisp, clean whites from clay schist soils; and the Società Industriale Immobiliare Carraresi (SIIC), producing intensely musky Colline di Candia dei Colli Apuani from Vermentino, Albarola, and Muscat grapes.

Route Two: Colline Lucchesi and Montecarlo

Begin in Colline Lucchesi by leaving Lucca on the road to Camaiore, crossing onto the left bank of the river Serchio at Monte San Quirico, taking signs towards San Concordio di Moriano for Sardi Giustiniani (see box, right; English spoken). The estate has been in the same family for over two centuries and produces wines typical of the low-lying hills here, soft-centred reds based on Sangiovese and French grapes, and clean, lush dry whites from Vermentino, Trebbiano, Grechetto, and Malvasia. There are seven comfortable, modern apartments, plus a villa for agritourism accommodation, too.

From Monte San Quirico follow the Serchio River north to cross onto the right bank at Ponte a Moriano and Fattoria Colle Verde (see box, right; by appointment, English spoken) in the hills at Matraia. This is one of the few estates in the Colline Lucchesi with its own olive oil press, albeit a modern one rather than a grindstone. The estate's olive groves and vines cover terraces known in local dialect as

Route One: Colline Apuani and Colli dei Luni
Allow two days

Route Two: Colline Lucchesi and Montecarlo
Allow two days

Route Three: Carmignano
Allow one or two days

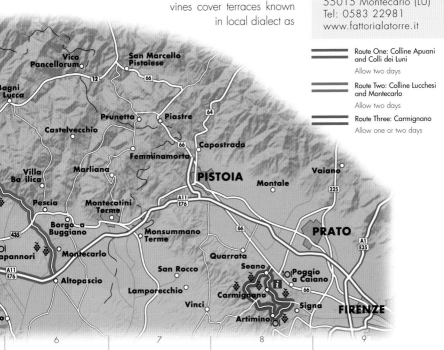

WHERE TO EAT

Osteria Il Vecchio Molino
Via Vittorio Emanuele, 12
55032 Castelnuovo di
Garfagnana (LU)
Tel: 0583 62192

Ristorante Da Delfina [A8]
Via della Chiesa, 1
59015 Artimino (PO)
Tel: 055 8718074

Ristorante Fontemorana [A8]
Via Fontemorana, 20
Loc Bacchereto
59015 Carmignano (PO)
Tel: 055 8717086

Ristorante Il Pinone [A8]
Via Montalbano, 16
59015 Carmignano (PO)
Tel: 055 8712094

**Trattoria Ristorante Il
Barco Reale [A8]**
Piazza Vittorio Emanuele II, 27
59015 Carmignano (PO)
Tel: 055 8711559

"Brania", a name commemorated on the label of Colle Verde's appealingly fresh and lightly oaked dry Trebbiano white, "Brania del Cancello" (*cancello* being a gate). Colle Verde is getting to grips with Syrah in its reds, with the 100% barrel-aged Syrah called "Nero della Spinosa" and the reassuringly peppery Sangiovese/Syrah blend "Brania del Ghiandaie".

Quantity can mean quality

From Matraia head across the hills to the hamlet of Valgiano and the Tenuta di Valgiano (*see* p.89; by appointment; English spoken). Unusually, in a wine sense, the largest vineyard in the zone is the area's top producer in terms of quality. Seventeen hectares of vines in a sun trap are watered by natural springs. Recent efforts in the vineyard by the Petrini family and hands-off winemaking in the cellars result in authentic, herb-scented dry whites like "Giallo dei Muri" from Vermentino (part barrel-fermented), Trebbiano, Malvasia, and Chardonnay, punchy reds like the Sangiovese, Syrah, and Merlot "Palistorti", and the pure Sangiovese "Scasso dei Cesari". The top red, bottled as "Tenuta di Valgiano", undergoes minimal pumping during its 18-month stay in barrel, reflected in its well-preserved floral tones and smooth fruit and mineral flavours.

Now cross into the Montecarlo zone by heading to La Torre (*see* p.89) just to the west of the town, in the shadow of Montecarlo's church bell tower. Since 1997 owner Elena Celli has tidied up the vineyards to get more even grape ripening, made her winery restaurant one of the best places to eat in Montecarlo, and is creating a reputation for solid Syrah reds like "Esse" and silky Sangiovese/Cabernet "Stringaio".

Slightly further west is the winery of Gino Fuso Carmignani (see p.89), known for thick dry Chardonnay and Roussanne whites, plus the weighty Syrah/Merlot/Sangiovese red "For Duke", a reference to Duke Ellington (the tasting room is covered in concert posters for the likes of Bob Dylan, Roy Orbison, and Tom Petty). The winery restaurant serves food in summer with fried chicken and potato a great reviver after a hard morning's wine tasting. Head back to Lucca by taking the Altopascio exit on the A11 motorway, direction Pisa.

Route Three: Carmignano

From the centre of Carmignano follow signs to Comeana, via the hamlet of La Serra, for Fattoria Ambra (see p.92; by appointment). The winery lies on the outskirts of Comeana (towards Poggio a Caiano) and, apart from a stainless-steel tank, looks more like a private house. Owner Giuseppe Rigoli's family bought the estate in 1870 and he now produces the most reliable and elegant range of Carmignano reds in the zone.

Rigoli's single-vineyard bottlings show the effect different soil types have here, with the clay-dominated "Elzana" vineyard producing a plump, thick red full of black plum fruit, and the "Santa Cristina in Pilli" vineyard, on sandier soil, producing reds with finer-grained tannins and lighter, more expressive fruit. Ambra's other single vineyard wines include "Vigna di Montefortine" and the "Vigne Alte Montalbiolo", two silky reds made from over two-thirds Sangiovese plus one-third Cabernet, Merlot, and Canaiolo vines planted in the early to mid-1970s.

From Comena head to the hamlet of Artimino for Fattoria di Artimino (see p.92; by appointment). The villa, built by the Medicis at the end of the 16th century, has an unmistakable roof, with dozens of chimney pots. The vineyards are surrounded in part by the famous "Barco Reale", the royal wall that protected the hunting forests of the Medici dukes, keeping animals like deer, boar, and rabbit in and poachers out. There are 700 hectares of land at the Artimino estate, around 10% of which is under vine. The cellars here are functional, and very little new oak is used, meaning the Artimino style is for soft, early drinking red wines under either the Barco Reale or Carmignano denominations. You can stay in the Artimino villa, called Villa Fernanda (it was built for Count Ferdinand de Medici), which has 50 apartments, and the

LEFT *Time for a few hoops before work.*

BELOW *Beautiful estates abound.*

WHERE TO STAY

Fabbrica di San Martino [A5]
Via Pieve S. Stefano, 2511
55100 San Martino in
Vignale (LU)
Tel: 0583 394284
www.fabbricadisanmartino.it

Macea Agriturismo [C5]
Loc Macea
55023 Borgo a Mozzano (LU)
Tel: 0583 88128

Montagna Verde [E2]
Via Appela, 1
54016 Licciana Narde (MS)
Tel: 0187 421203
www.agriturismoborgoantico.com

Saudon Agriturismo [F2]
Via Madonna del Monte, 7
Loc Monteguzzo
54026 Pozzo di Mulazzo (MS)
Tel: 0187 439679
www.agriturismosaudon.it

WINERIES IN CARMIGNANO

Fattoria Ambra [A8]
Via Lombardia, 85
59015 Carmignano (PO)
Tel: 0554 86488
fattoria.ambra@libero.it

Fattoria di Artimino [A8]
Fraz Artimino, 59015
Carmignano (PO)
Tel: 055 8792051
artimino@tin.it

Fattoria di Bacchereto [A8]
Via Fontemorana, 179
59015 Bacchereto (PO)
Tel: 055 8717191
fattoriadibacchereto@libero.it

Pratesi [A8]
Loc Seano, Via Rizzelli, 10
59011 Carmignano (PO)
Tel: 0558 706400

Tenuta di Capezzana [A8]
Loc Capezzana
59015 Carmignano (PO)
Tel: 055 8706005/6091
www.capezzana.it

estate also runs two restaurants called Biagio Pignatta and La Cantine del Redi, with hare, kid, and duck the specialties.

From Artimino head to the hamlet of Bacchereto, for the emerging Fattoria di Bacchereto (*see* box, left). Surrounded by olive groves and woodland, the vineyards are tucked into the hills on narrow terraces. This is also one of the few Carmignano estates that you can visit at weekends, although do call ahead to make sure someone will be there to receive you. Rosella Bencini Tesi now runs this family property, used as a hunting lodge during the Medici period (part of the Barco Reale wall cuts across Bacchereto). Rosella is adopting Biodynamic methods to "get back to basics"; working with lunar cycles to cut down on vineyard sprays and the need for filtration in the wines. Bacchereto is now producing reds with super-bright flavours of plum and violet as well as an unctuous dry white from Malvasia and Trebbiano. You can stay in five farmhouse apartments here (30 rooms in total, plus swimming pool), and buy delicious olive oil, dried figs, and chestnut flour produced on the estate, too.

From here head back towards Carmignano for Capezzana hamlet and the Tenuta di Capezzana (*see* box, left). The villa dates from the 14th century, and features long, winding underground cellars and a bright tasting room/shop. Owners the Contini-Bonacossi family replanted some of their Cabernet Sauvignon vines with cuttings from Bordeaux's famous Château Lafite-Rothschild, but Capezzana's reds today are made in a soft, southern Mediterranean style. *See* the website for details of Capezzanna's cookery school.

Near Capezzana, in the direction of Seano, is the emerging estate of Pratesi (*see* box, left), producing toasty, dark coloured reds like Locorosso (90% Sangiovese with 10% Merlot). Head back to Carmignano, visiting the friendly Castelvecchio winery (www.castelvecchio.net) on the way.

San Gimignano

Two million tourists are said to pound the streets of San Gimignano each year, drawn by the town's remarkable skyline. San Gimignano is a medieval Manhattan, its 57 towers, now reduced to 14, created as much for military purposes between feuding religious factions of Guelphs and Ghibellines as by the vanity of local noblemen. Historians have yet to ascertain whether the height of each tower was proportionately related to the nobleman's wealth, or inversely proportionate to the size of his manhood.

Appealing to the masses

Locals complain that due to this influx of tourists local wineries and restaurateurs don't have to try too hard to make a sale. It is true that there is not a single restaurant of ultra-high quality in the town; you have to go to the Michelin-starred Arnolfo in Colle di Val d'Elsa for that.

As for wine, San Gimignano's production – from less than 900 hectares within the communal boundary – is inevitably destined for its uncritical and captive tourist market, and white wines from the Vernaccia dominate. So, if you are of the opinion that Tuscany's white wines run a poor second to the reds, and that the Vernaccia grape upon which San Gimignano has pinned its reputation is of only moderate quality, you'd best stick to the area's often surprisingly good red wines, either Chianti Colli Senesi, as San Gimignano is part of this Chianti sub-zone (see Siena chapter), or San Gimignano Rosso, both of which contain at least 70% Sangiovese.

No one quite knows the origins of San Gimignano's Vernaccia, but it has been grown here since at least 1276, and it is known to be different from the grape of the same name found in Liguria and Sardinia. The wine is commonly described as tasting varnish-like, which could account for its name. The grape has a reputation for providing full-bodied white wines with stinging acidic freshness, flavours of flint, crab apple, bitter almonds, liquorice, and even violets, and a marked off-yellow colour. In the hands of good growers, like the Falchinis of Casale, Montenidoli, Vagnoni, Panizzi, and La Rampa di Fugnano, Vernaccia can be like a more highly flavoured and assertive version of Chardonnay, but with more obvious wine-like flavour. Purists lament the fact that Vernaccia, which was 100% varietal from San Gimignano, can now contain 10% Chardonnay, as idiotic a decision as asking the keepers of San Gimignano's towers to renovate them using Plexiglass or corrugated iron on the "why not, everyone else is using it" principle.

LEFT *The Barco Reale wall survives the test of time.*

LOCAL INFORMATION

Consorzio della Denominazione San Gimignano [C3]
Via Villa della Rocca, 1
53037 San Gimignano (SI)
Tel: 0577 940108
info@vernaccia.it
www.vernaccia.it
The Vernaccia di San Gimignano wine-growers' consortium was originally founded in the 1970s, but appeared not too dynamic until it was restructured in the mid-1990s. The growers have now produced a map showing the location of around 80 member wineries.

Ufficio Turistico [C3]
Piazza Duomo, 1
53037 San Gimignano (SI)
Tel: 0577 940008
www.sangimignano.com
The San Gimignano tourist office is one of Italy's busiest – so be patient!

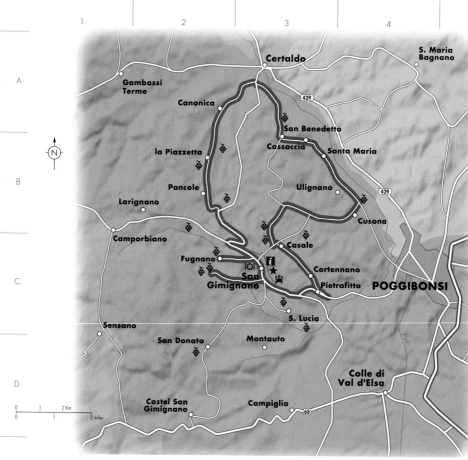

Vernaccia di San Gimignano

Siena(Chianti Colli Senesi)

Florence (Chianti Colli Fiorentini) and Montespertoli

Route: San Gimignano
Allow two days

Getting there
By car, exit at Poggibonsi Nord from the Siena–Florence dual carriageway, and follow signs for San Gimignano. The nearest railway station is Poggibonsi. Bus services are run by SITA.

Travelling around
Route summary From San Gimignano head east towards Poggibonsi, doubling back at Fornace for Casale. Then travel east to Cusona, northwest to Ulignano, past Santa Maria and San Benedetto towards Certaldo, then back to San Gimignano via Pancole, with detours to Fugnano and Montenidoli. The route length is about 35km (21 miles). Allow a couple of days.

Route: San Gimignano
From the centre of San Gimignano head south from the Porta San Giovanni, turning left at the first roundabout in the direction of Poggibonsi, Colle Val d'Elsa, Florence, and Siena.

Canneta is signposted (see p.98; no coaches) on the right up a narrow dirt track. Owner Stefano Grandi offers free visits (English spoken) with no obligation to buy. With his partner Valeria Bevilacqua, Stefano farms around six hectares of mainly

Vernaccia vineyards organically. Instead of fungicides, plant extracts mixed with clay are sprayed on the grapes to act as a barrier against fungal disease spores. The clay helps the plant extracts to stick to the grape skins.

Canneta's vineyards are on quite steep slopes, so grass is maintained between the rows to prevent erosion and encourage beneficial insects like ladybirds, to keep pests at bay. The unprepossessing winery is sited partially outside, but Grandi's wines show good consistency.

Two Vernaccia di San Gimignanos are made: the entry-level "Canneta" which mixes nuts, lime, and pineapple; and a *riserva* called "La Luna e le Torri" ("the moon and the towers") part-fermented in French barrels, giving it more depth. The oak-aged "Fiore Rosso" Sangiovese, with a dash of Canaiolo, Colorino, and Merlot, shows crisp, clean, tight-grained fruit.

Grandi is helping his near-neighbour, Simone Santini of Tenuta Le Calcinaie (*see*, p.98) to convert to organic growing. Santini planted his first vines in 1986 and, apart from Grandi's help, is very much a one-man band, so call ahead if you want to visit. The wine style here is similar to Canneta, although as the Santini vines are younger than Canneta's the wines are slightly lighter.

You can walk back to San Gimignano from Canneta, not by road, but by the Imboltroni River (you'll need sturdy boots). It takes around two hours but you can swim in rock pools and under waterfalls on the way.

EXTRA INFORMATION

For information on the local saffron producers contact "The Crocus Association":

Associazione Il Croco [C3]
Via delle Fonti, 3/a
53037 San Gimignano (SI)
Tel: 0577 940986
prolocsg@tin.it

BELOW *The towering skyline of San Gimignano.*

ABOVE *The narrow winding streets of San Gimignano.*

Keep going to Poggibonsi, and half-way between San Gimignano and Poggibonsi turn sharp left at Fornace in the direction of Pietrafitta for the Fattoria di Pietrafitta at Località Cortennano (tel: 0577 943200; www.pietrafitta.com).

The older the better

This is one of the zone's longest established producers, and the vineyards, containing some of the oldest vines in San Gimignano, were planted by an elderly countess. Older vintages can age quite beautifully – the 1974 had a lovely soft waxy feel with bright honey and butter flavours when 30 years old, testament that Vernaccia can age as well as most red grapes, thanks to its marked level of acidity. In contrast, a 1987, tasted when only 17 years old, was fading fast, perhaps a sign that the vineyards were being gradually more intensively farmed and for higher yields.

Pietrafitta perhaps no longer enjoys the reputation it once did for its wines, but you can buy bottles from their stall at the side of the (unsurfaced) road and enjoy a picnic on your way to the Falchini family's Casale estate.

Before you get there you will see on your left the best views of San Gimignano's towers; and as this road is one few tourists are aware of, and is essentially inaccessible to larger vehicles like coaches, it is quiet too, so you can take your time. The odd, forgotten, rusting tractor provides a contrasting foreground to San Gimignano's dramatic skyline, testament to how much less durable are modern human inventions.

Mixing up the grapes

At the end of the road, turn right in the direction of San Andrea and the Azienda Agricola Casale (*see* p.98) appears on the left. San Gimignano is 1.5km (1 mile) to the south. The old *casale* or farmhouse here was once inhabited by friars, but in the 1960s Riccardo Falchini, a construction engineer from Prato, renovated it and then set about planting vineyards. Crucially, instead of clonally selecting his vines, he took a mix of cuttings from the best local vineyards. This means that instead of having a vineyard of one clone with just one flavour profile, Falchini planted a mix. So in his vineyards, while some vines produce big berries giving good quantities of juice, others produce much smaller berries which give more concentrated flavour plus a richer, deeper colour and much more complex-tasting wines.

Falchini's Vernaccia "Vigna a Solatio", or "sunny-site vineyard", is made with some late-picked, overripe grapes which gives one of the most intense and distinctively varnish-like white wines of the region. Other white wines made here include a delicious, biscuity sparkling blend of Vernaccia, Pinot Noir, and Chardonnay and a powerful, savoury *vin santo* made from Malvasia and Trebbiano. Some of the *vin santo* barrels were used to age bourbon at the former US military base, Camp Darby, near Pisa.

All Falchini's red wines show soft, smooth fruit flavours. "Campora", a French oak aged Cabernet Sauvignon with a bit of Merlot, is rightly considered one of Tuscany's top Bordeaux blends. Visitors can buy wine without making an appointment, but book ahead if you want to see the cellars as the winery buildings are small and in several locations.

The big players
Just up the road from Falchini is Bruna Baroncini's Cantine Baroncini (see p.99). Along with big merchants like Cecchi, Melini, and Zonin this is one of the bigger players in the zone.

Baroncini's Vernaccia bottlings "Poggio ai Cannici Sovestro" and "Dometaia" are, like her cellars, competent rather than inspiring. Solid, not entirely graceless red wines are made, with the San Gimignano Rosso "Il Casato" and Chianti Colli Senesi "Vigna San Domenico Sovestro" the most notable.

Another, much smaller producer in Casale is Giovanni Leoncini's Capella Sant'Andrea (tel: 0577 940456). Vernaccia di San Gimignano under the Capella Sant'Andrea and Rialto labels taste best after a good airing in the glass.

From Casale you can bear left towards Certaldo and San Andrea where the emerging Mormoraia (www.mormoraia.it) winery is found; but we bear right towards Ulignano and the hamlet of Mattone. Here the landscape is softer as the land rolls towards Poggibonsi and the valley of the Elsa River. On the way to Mattone you pass Teruzzi e Puthod's Fattoria Ponte a Rondolino (see p.99; open daily, with coach parking). This is one of the San Gimignano domains that put modern Vernaccia on the map, with a gleaming James Bond-esque winery.

Enrico Terruzi and his French ballerina wife Carmen Puthod arrived here in 1974 and by the 1980s were producing unashamedly modern white wines, using cool fermentation in stainless-steel tanks to make clean wines with plenty of tropical flavours to complement the Vernaccia grape's oilier, more varnish-like side. They also used fermentation in new oak barrels for their top Vernaccia di San Gimignano, the *riserva* "Terre di Tufo", which was described by excited wine critics in the early 1990s as the "Rolls-Royce of Vernaccias". However, even though Terruzi e Puthod still produce reliable whites, the red wines such as the Sangiovese bottling called "Peperino" have never consistently hit the heights. Other Vernaccia producers like

WINERIES IN SAN GIMIGNANO

Azienda Agricola Canneta [C3]
Via Località San Lucia, 27
53037 San Gimignano (SI)
Tel: 0577 941540
canneta@supereva.it
www.canneta.supereva.it

Azienda Agricola Casale [C3] (Falchini)
Loc Casale
53037 San Gimignano (SI)
Tel: 0577 941305 (winery)
or 0574 28123 (office)
casalefalchini@tin.it

Tenuta Le Calcinaie [C3]
Loc Santa Lucia, 36
53036 San Gimignano (SI)
Tel: 0577 943007

Montenidoli and Casale (Falchini) seem to draw more flavour and texture from their grapes than Terruzi e Puthod.

From Mattone keep going east towards Cusona. At the far eastern edge of the zone is the Fattoria Cusona, owned by the Guicciardini-Strozzi family (see p.99), cousins of the Guicciardini at the Castello di Poppiano in Chianti Colli Fiorentini.

Power and influence, for a fee

The 15th-century villa, made of local sandstone, and the early 19th-century gardens played host to British Prime Minister Tony Blair and his family in the late 1990s. Wine has been made here since the 10th century, and the long, cavernous cellars, lit by flickering bulbs on cobwebbed wires powered by almost lever-like switches, are certainly atmospheric.

Cusona charges a not inconsiderable fee for a visit, but you can taste four wines from the large range. The owners have vineyards in Bolgheri on the Etruscan coast, and in Monteregio di Massa Marittima and Scansano in Grosseto, as well as San Gimignano.

With vineyards in so many locations, Cusona successfully blends grapes into generic (IGT) Tuscan wines like the chunky "Millanni" (60% Sangiovese and 40% Cabernet Sauvignon/Merlot). Varietal wines like "Selvascura" (100% Merlot) and "Sòdole" (100% Sangiovese) wear their flavours of oak well. Several Vernaccias are made in a clean, fresh style, including a herby, barrel-fermented *riserva*, the single-vineyard "San Biagio", and the simpler unoaked "Titolato".

BELOW *Azienda Agricola Canneta is San Gimignano's pioneering organic winery.*

From Cusona head northwest and parallel with the Pesa River through the hamlets of Ulignano and Santa Maria following signs to Certaldo.

The Santa Maria area has a reputation as something of a bulk-wine backwater thanks to the Lucii Libanio brothers, producing wine sold by the tanker, rather than by the bottle. This part of San Gimignano is flattish and easy to farm, so high yields are tempting to growers.

Easy drinking

In Santa Maria, you'll find Fontaleoni, source of well-constructed Vernaccia like the "Vigna Casa Nuova". The vineyards were planted in the 1970s at a low density of less than 3,000 vines per hectare as opposed to the modern trend of 5,000 per hectare. Generally speaking, higher density vineyards are said to produce more concentrated vines, as each vine has to bear fewer grapes than in a lower density system. However, Fontaleoni's wines are a good example of how low density vineyards can provide easy drinking if the wines are made in a no-fuss style for early consumption.

Continue past Santa Maria to reach the hamlet of San Benedetto and the emerging winery of Il Lebbio (see box, right). Here the Niccolini brothers produce a number of succulent red wines from various blends. These include "Grottoni" from Cabernet, Merlot, and Montepulciano, which seems to ripen well on the sandy soils in this part of the San Gimignano zone; "Polito", from Sangiovese and Colorino, which needs plenty of air in the glass before drinking; and the agreeably juicy-fruit-styled "Cicogio" from Ciliegiolo, Colorino, and Sangiovese.

From Il Lebbio continue to the hamlet of Casaccia and then through the hamlet of San Benedetto. At the T-junction turn right, direction Certaldo, and then almost immediately left via the hamlets of Canonica and La Piazzetta to Pancole.

Around La Piazzetta

Before you reach La Piazzetta on the right-hand side Casa alle Vacche (see p.102) is signposted. Owned by the Ciappi brothers, football-mad Fernando and his quieter sibling Lorenzo, Casa alle Vacche has a comfortable, large tasting room. The winery enjoys a tranquil location in the hills that make the Pancole zone renowned. Cereal crops, as well as olives, are grown, and there is plenty of woodland for guests to go walking. The Ciappis produce appealing whites, but their Chianti Colli Senesi reds offer perhaps the best value.

Just south of La Piazzetta is Vagnoni (see box, right), a family estate run by Luigi Vagnoni, regarded by his peers as one of the best wine-growers in the San Gimignano zone. Vagnoni's parents bought the estate in the early 1950s when land prices

WINERIES IN SAN GIMIGNANO (CONTINUED)

Bruna Baroncini [C3]
Loc Casale, 43
53037 San Gimignano (SI)
Tel: 0577 940600

Ca' del Vispo [C2]
Loc Le Vigne
Via di Fugnano, 31
53037 San Gimignano (SI)
Tel: 0577 943053
cadelvispo@libero.it

Fattoria Ponte a Rondolino [B2] Loc Casale, 19
53037 San Gimignano (SI)
Tel: 0577 9401343

Guicciardini-Strozzi [B4]
Loc Cusona, 5
53037 San Gimignano (SI)
Tel: 0577 950028
www.guicciardinistrozzi.it

Il Lebbio [A3]
Loc San Benedetto, 11/C
53037 San Gimignano (SI)
Tel: 0577 944725
illebbio@libero.it

Montenidoli [B2]
Loc Montenidoli
53037 San Gimignano (SI)
Tel: 0577 941565
www.montenidoli.com

Panizzi [B2]
Loc Racciano, 34
Fraz Santa Margherita
53037 San Gimignano (SI)
Tel: 0577 941576
www.panizzi.it

La Rampa di Fugnano [C2]
Loc Fugnano, 55
53037 San Gimignano (SI)
Tel: 0577 941655
www.rampadifugnano.it

San Quirico [B2]
Loc Pancole, 39
53037 San Gimignano (SI)
Tel: 0577 955007
az.agr.sanquirico@libero.it

Vagnoni [C3]
Fraz Pancole, 82
53037 San Gimignano (SI)
Tel: 0577 955077

ABOVE *Rolling hills, a single cypress, a terracotta roof, and endless vines...*

were cheap due to rural depopulation. Gradually more land was added, and the vineyards expanded to include some of the best sites in the San Gimignano zone for Vernaccia, with perfect south and southwest exposure and just the right soils. The height above sea level is also critical, around 250 metres (820 feet), meaning temperatures are steady enough to allow the grapes to ripen slowly.

Vagnoni's top label, the "Riserva Mocale" has a firm core, but its dry stone fruit flavours soften into something more waxy after three to five years in bottle. Reliable Chianti Colli Senesi reds are also made, and IGT Toscana "I Sodi Lungi" an oak-aged Sangiovese/Colorino/Merlot blend.

Keeping it in the family

Continue in the direction of Pancole, passing through the village, after which you'll see a left-hand turn to San Quirico (see p.99). Owner Andrea Vecchione's great-grandfather bought the land in 1860, his grandfather built the house in 1900, and he bottled his first wines here in 1970. Organic manure is applied to the soil, and weeds are ploughed out rather than sprayed. Vecchione also has a plot of crocuses for saffron. The winery is pretty rustic, but visitors are welcome and wine tastings are free. San Quirico's San Gimignano Rosso "Botticello" shows how winemakers in white wine regions are often tempted to make red wines with the same lightness of touch. Whites here comprise a basic Vernaccia and two *riservas*, the single-vineyard "I Campi Santi" and "Isabella", named after Vecchione's daughter. It is fermented in large wooden oval vats (*botti*) and left for six months on the yeast to soften Vernaccia's sometimes aggressive acid.

Carry on to San Gimignano from Pancole, turning right to the hamlet of Fugnano. The leading estate here, La Rampa di Fugnano (see pp.100 and 102) is owned by a Swiss couple, former school teacher Gisela Traxler and former IBM sales director Herbert Ehrenbold (call ahead for visits; English spoken). They bought the estate in 1990 and their first harvest, the severely frost-hit 1991, taught them just how hard wine-growing could be. Ultra-low density vineyards at just 1,500 vines per hectare were replanted at 6,000–7,000 per hectare, to get proportionately fewer, and thus more concentrated, grapes.

A very distinctive range of wines is produced. Bright peach tones are evident in both the Vernaccia di San Gimignano called "Alata" and the *riserva* "Privato", which is part-fermented in older wood. A Viognier, "Viognié", shows exotic dried fruit. All of the white wines are carefully hand-picked and only ultra-low levels of wine preservative (SO_2) are used. Red wines include a delicious Merlot "Gisèle", a wild, scented Sangiovese "Bomboreto", and a generous (and good value) Chianti Colli Senesi "Via dei Franchi".

Partners in wine

From Fugnano go back towards the Certaldo–San Gimignano road but stop at the reliable Ca' del Vispo (*see* p.99) on the left-hand side. This is a partnership between Roberto Vispi, who is from Trentino, and the Tuscan dal Din family. White wines ferment in stainless-steel tanks, with reds fermented in lined cement tanks, which are coming back into fashion as they retain the heat needed for good extraction of colour from the skins.

Ca' del Vispo produces a solid Chianti Colli Senesi and a softer red from Sangiovese and Colorino called "Poggio Solivo". The "Fondatore" red made from 50% Cabernet Franc and 50% Cabernet Sauvignon shows off the former's violet flavours well. The 100% Merlot "Cruter" is deliberately made in a jammy style by leaving the berries partly uncrushed when they go into the vat. A barrel-fermented dry white wine, "Segümo", made from Chardonnay plus Pinot Grigio and Sauvignon Blanc, shows that interesting San Gimignano white wines do not have to revolve just around Vernaccia.

Once back on the Certaldo–San Gimignano road, skirt around the western outskirts of San Gimignano until you reach the Montemaggio car park. Turn right, following the track between the police station (*carabinieri*) and the car park to reach the Panizzi winery (*see* p.99). Owner Giovanni Panizzi, a computing specialist from Milan, bought the estate in 1979 when there was just one hectare. Panizzi has created a good reputation for his wines – his are among the most expensive Vernaccia di San Gimignano on the market. Panizzi favours the lyre training system, so the vine canopy is divided in two at the top. This allows more sunlight into the canopy improving ripeness and helping prevent disease; but it also means the vines must be expensively hand-picked.

This extra ripeness shows in Panizzi's Vernaccia di San Gimignano and the single-vineyard *riserva*, "Vigna Santa Margherita". Rather than fermenting this *riserva* in barrel, Panizzi starts the fermentation off in tank and then moves the fermenting juice to barrel. His use of oak is equally assured in the Chianti Colli Senesi "Vertunno", named after the god Vertunnus, who presides over the change of the seasons.

WHERE TO STAY

Il Casale del Cotone [C3]
Loc Cellole, 59
53037 San Gimignano (SI)
Tel: 0577 943236
info@casaledelcotone.com
www.casaledelcotone.com
Traditionally furnished double and triple rooms, plus apartments, with an atmospheric courtyard. Breakfast included, dinner extra.

Montenidoli [C3]
Loc Montenidoli
53037 San Gimignano (SI)
Tel: 0577 941565
elisabetta@montenidoli.com
www.montenidoli.com
Isolated agritourism apartments with all rooms having bathrooms and TV; good service (towels provided and changed daily) plus a meeting centre for groups, swimming pool, tennis, bowls – and great wine.

Podere Il Caggiolino [C3]
Loc Picchena
53030 Castel San Gimignano (SI)
Tel: 0577 953190
caggiolino@gmx.net
www.caggiolino.com
Bed and breakfast; double rooms with bathroom, lounge and terrace; peaceful location amongst olive groves and vineyards.

Il Vecchio Maneggio [C3]
Loc San Andrea, 22
Ulignano
53037 San Gimignano (SI)
Tel: 0577 950232
info@ilvecchiomaneggio.com
www.ilvecchiomaneggio.com
An organic estate which offers rooms to rent, rustic country dinners, and pony trekking. Kids are welcome.

WHERE TO STAY

Casa alle Vacche [C3]
Fraz Pancole
Loc Lucignano, 73/A
53037 San Gimignano (SI)
Tel: 0577 955103
casaallevacche@
cybermarket.it
Seven peaceful self-
catering apartments
(two for four people
and five for two people)
open all year. Swimming
pool and views to San
Gimignano's towers.

La Rampa di Fugnano [C3]
Loc Fugnano, 55
53037 San Gimignano (SI)
Tel: 0577 941655
info@rampadifugnano.it
www.rampadifugnano.it
High quality, modern,
self-catering apartment
with lovely views east
towards San Gimignano
and southeast towards
the Montenidoli winery
and the Fugnano Valley.
Also has a car park in
a gated compound.

BELOW *Polyculture in action:
artichokes grow amid the vines.*

Maritime influence

Carry on up the very bumpy track from Panizzi to reach winemaker Maria Elisabetta Fagiuoli and her poet husband Sergio d'Asej's Montenidoli (see p.99; by appointment). The name means "hill of the birds' nests" and when Fagiuoli has taken you to her highest vineyards (650 metres/2,132 feet) you can see why. The vineyard soil ranges from land littered with sea shells dating from 50 million years ago, where the pale-coloured soil suits the Vernaccia, to more mineral-rich red soils dating from 250 million years ago higher up. This suits red wines, so Syrah vines have been planted, fenced off from marauding wild boar.

Fagiuoli bought the estate in 1965, when it was completely abandoned. There is no signpost for Montenidoli, but these are among the most mineral-rich and complex wines in the zone. Excellent pruning, old vines, naturally low yields, and careful picking contribute to Montenidoli's inherent complexity. These wines need time in bottle to show their best, running counter to modern San Gimignano wineries where supplying easy-drinking wines to tourists is the norm.

At Montenidoli this applies equally to red and white wines, the most obvious example being the defiantly traditional Sangiovese-based "Sono Montenidoli". Its name means "I am Montenidoli". In other words the wine tastes of the place it comes from. "Here, the style is the land," says Fagiuoli. The Vernaccias have real purity and freshness in their youth, and become earthy, less overt with age. Montenidoli's unfiltered olive oil is one of Tuscany's best.

A few extras

You can head back to San Gimignano the way you came. As a footnote, south of the town on the road to Castel San Gimignano and not on our wine route, turn left for the hamlet of Racciano and Claudia Galgani's tiny Podere Le Volute (tel: 0577 97278), source of very good organic olive oil. Fruity Chianti Colli Senesi and Novello reds are produced.

Further south on the Castel San Gimignano road, at San Donato, is the Lenzi family's visitor-friendly Fattoria San Donato (tel: 0577 941616), with simple wines offering good value, as well as olive oil, grain, and sunflowers (for oil). Another good stop is on the Via per Castel San Gimignano is Monica Rota and Giorgio Comotti's Il Palagione (tel: 0577 953134; palagione@tin.it) if you like a Vernaccia with real bite.

On the very edge of the San Gimignano zone you'll find the powerful merchant Zonin's Fattoria Il Palagio Zonin (tel: 0577 953004; www.ilpalagio.it), the largest San Gimignano estate with 120 hectares under vine. Whites are more successful than reds; "La Gentilesca" is the most reliable.

Montalcino and Brunello

The hilltop town of Montalcino is an unlikely wine mecca, its people as austere as its famous unique red Brunello wines. Montalcino has always had something of a siege mentality, more comfortable doing things its own way rather than to the tune of other towns like Florence and Siena, which fought for control here until the 1550s. The approach to the town is barren, whether you arrive from the north through the lunar-like landscape of the *crete senesi* and Siena, or from the south across the banks of the Orcia and the surrounding dry woodland scrub.

From acorns, mighty oaks

Montalcino owes its name to "oak tree mountain" after the oak trees (*ilex*) that thrive around its mountainous hill ("*Mons Ilicini*" or Montalcino), and whose tannin was used to tan leather in the Middle Ages (the oak trees were burnt at kilns or "*le fornace*" for tile-making).

The town owes its modern day wine fame to the Biondi-Santi family who, in the late 19th century, isolated a dark brown, small-berried and especially potent strain of the Sangiovese grape which they called Brunello, or "the little dark one", and Brunello di Montalcino was born. After several cycles of boom and bust, Montalcino's 100% Sangiovese (*ergo* Brunello) wines are among the most expensive in Italy. The quality difference between the supermarket-style Brunello of Banfi, Col d'Orcia, Val di Suga, and Castelgiocondo and the carefully crafted Brunello of producers like Salicutti, Roberto Bellini, Sesti, and La Torre should convince you that one of the most ruinous mistakes potential purchasers of Brunello wine can make is to fail to research what they are buying first.

Blending in flavour

One problem is that, although everyone knows what Brunello should taste like – fruits like black cherry and plum, flowers like violet or even tulip, and with a firm, fresh core of mouth-coating blackberry tannins – few care to deny that many modern Brunellos taste as if other grapes have been added in. Cabernet (blackcurrants), Merlot (raspberry), or even Nero d'Avola (leather) can all be planted in the region, but are not supposed to be blended into Brunello di Montalcino. Instead they must be used in minor red wines labelled Sant'Antimo (after a local abbey), which require no Sangiovese at all.

Another problem with Brunello is that it must age for several years (the rules keep changing) in wood before sale, which ups

LOCAL INFORMATION

Consorzio del Vino Brunello di Montalcino [B3]
Costa del Municipio, 1
53024 Montalcino (SI)
Tel: 0577 848246
consbrun@tin.it
www.consorzio
brunellodimontalcino.it
This consortium is well organized and produces an excellent (free) map marking producers and their contact details. Open daily. Don't visit during the "Benvenuto Brunello" in mid-February when the producers totally focus on showing the newly released wines to trade buyers.

Ufficio Turistico Comunale/Azienda Promozione Turistica [B3]
Costa del Municipio, 8
53024 Montalcino (SI)
Tel: 0577 849331
Closed Monday.
Helpful for general tourist enquiries, but go next door to the Consorzio del Vino Brunello di Montalcino (see above) for any queries that are wine specific. Provides details on local events.

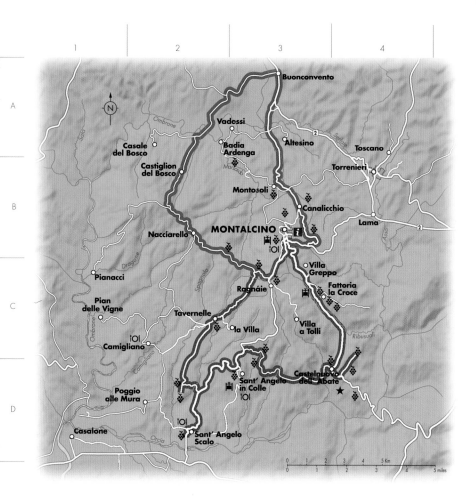

Montalcino

Route One: Montalcino north
Allow two days

Route Two: Montalcino south
Allow two days

its price as producers have to sit on huge stocks. *Riservas* age longest of all; the ageing period in wood allows Brunello's harsh tannins to soften. Cheaper reds from the Brunello grape are sold as Rosso di Montalcino. They offer especially good value from lesser vintage years when the best Brunello grapes are declassified into Rosso di Montalcino for cashflow, as Rosso must age less than half as long as Brunello before it can be sold. Only a few producers make the sweet, late-picked, and sometimes diverting white called Moscadello.

Getting there

By car Montalcino is easily reached on the SS2 Siena–Viterbo –Rome road (the Via Cassia), about 40km (25 miles) south of Siena and 86km (55 miles) north of Viterbo.

By bus there are regular services to Montalcino via Buonconvento from Siena's Piazza Gramsci with a company called TRAIN SpA (see www.trainspa.it for details). Journey time is around one hour.

Montalcino's hilltop location means there is no railway station. The nearest railway stations are at Buonconvento to the north and Stazione di Sant'Angelo-Cinigiano to the south.

Travelling around

Route summaries There are two possible itineraries for the Montalcino region.

Route One summary Around 50km (30miles) in length, this covers the northern half of the Montalcino zone, in a circle from Montalcino itself via Castiglion del Bosco and the town of Buonconvento and back to Montalcino. Allow a couple of days.

Route Two summary This route covers the southern half of Montalcino, via Castelnuovo dell'Abate, Sant'Angelo in Colle, Sant'Angelo Scalo, Argiano, Tavernelle, and back to Montalcino. Around 48km (30 miles) in length, so again, allow a couple of days.

Route One: Montalcino north

From the roundabout by Montalcino's fortress (*fortezza*) go straight across, direction Grosseto.

Wineries appearing on the left-hand side include the rather old-fashioned Tornesi, Villa I Cipressi (www.villacipressi.it), whose owners, the Ciacci family, produce well-constructed Brunellos with a blackcurrant core and a range of scented honeys; Bellaria (tel: 0577 848574) near the hotel of that name, which offers free tastings of its ephemeral wines; and San Lucia (see p.110), whose Rosso and Brunello di Montalcino show good levels of ripeness and weight of fruit, plus notable clarity, from well-selected grapes at picking.

Wineries appearing on the right-hand side include the rather simple Canneta, and next door the emerging Brunelli (see p.107). Luca Brunelli planted 3.5 hectares of Sangiovese as soon as he finished his studies in 1996, whilst working in local vineyards. His red wines age in small barriques and larger *botti*, and show generously ripe fruit and smooth tannins.

Also here are Tenuta Vitanza (tel: 0577 846031, www.tenutavitanza.it), producing around 30,000 bottles of clean, elegant, and reassuringly simple reds (not to be confused with the nearby winery called Vitanza), Pietroso, whose wines are marked by flavours of old wood, Terralsole, and Il Palazzone, whose reds are rather lean.

After 3.2km (2 miles) take the first right, direction Argiano, Camigliano, and Tavernelle. Ignore the first sign left to Argiano and continue towards Castiglion del Bosco. The first winery on the right after the road becomes unsurfaced is Il Poggiolo (see p.106), not to be confused with Il Poggione (see Route Two). Il Poggiolo's owner Rodolfo (Rudy) Cosimi makes classic-tasting,

(see p.110)
(see p.107)
(see p.106)

WHERE TO STAY

Agriturismo Le Benducce
Loc Le Benducce
53024 Montalcino (SI)
Tel: 0577 848665
benducce@yahoo.it
An apartment, pool, bicycle hire, and atmospheric setting.

Il Paradiso di Frassina
Loc Paradiso di Frassina
53024 Montalcino (SI)
Tel: 0577 839031
alparadiso@tiscalinet.it
www.alparadisodifrassina.it
Quiet apartment overlooked by the Montalcino hill.

Piombaia
Loc Piombaia, 230
53024 Montalcino (SI)
Tel: 0577 848645
piombaia@piombaia.com
www.piombaia.com
Winery with restaurant and holiday home.

Salicutti
Loc Podere Salicutti, 174
53024 Montalcino (SI)
Tel: 0577 847003
leanza@poderesalicutti.it
www.poderesalicutti.it
Two simple but characterful apartments plus pool on a beautiful estate.

San Polino
Podere San Polino, 163
53024 Montalcino (SI)
Tel: 0577 835775
vino@sanpolino.it
www.sanpolino.it
Small but comfortable apartment with terrace and super views.

Tenuta di Argiano
Loc Sant'Angelo in Colle, 74
53024 Montalcino (SI)
Tel: 0577 844037
argiano@argiano.net
www.argiano.net
Two secluded guesthouses sleeping up to 18 people plus private garden and pool with superb views.

WINERIES IN MONTALCINO

. . . .
PRICES: moderate to expensive

**Azienda Agraria
Fossacolle [C2]**
Loc Tavernelle, 7
53024 Montalcino
Tel: 0577 816013

Fuligni [B2]
Via Soccorso Saloni, 32
53024 Montalcino (SI)
Tel: 0577 848039

Il Paradiso di Manfredi [B2]
Loc Il Paradiso di Manfredi
53024 Montalcino (SI)
Tel: 0577 848748

Il Poggiolo [B2]
Loc Il Poggiolo, 259
53024 Montalcino (SI)
Tel: 0577 848412
www.ilpoggiolomontalcino.com

Il Poggione [D3]
Fraz Sant'Angelo in Colle
Piazza Castello, 14
53024 Montalcino (SI)
Tel: 0577 844029
www.tenutailpoggione.it

vibrant Brunello di Montalcinos. Top selections like "Beato" show rich fruit flavours enhanced rather than drowned by a lavish oak topping. Cosimi's grappas are also agreeably understated.

Continue for 1.8km (1.1 miles) for a great view of the western slopes of Montalcino and the Ombrone Valley. Wineries here include Villa Le Prata (www.villaleprata.com), whose reds are very smoky from ageing in new oak barrels; the simpler Il Forteto (www.ilforteto.it); and the Gorelli family's Le Potazzine (see p.109). Soon the grand, cypress-lined entrance of Tenuta Corte Pavone (see p.111) appears on the right.

Biodynamic and organic wine-growing

Corte Pavone was purchased in 1996 by the Loacker family, who already owned the organic Schwarhof in Alto Adige, and whose name is one of the famous biscuit brands in south-central Europe. Organic and Biodynamic wine-growing has brought life back to the stony soils. Particularly vibrant Sangiovese, Cabernet Sauvignon, and Merlot reds like "Brillando" are made in a well-designed and visitor-friendly winery.

Continue through woodland for 2km (1.3 miles) past the Biondi-Santi family's Villa Poggio Salvi (bsanti@sienanet.it), which is slowly improving as the wines become more harmonized with the new oak barrels. Go past a small memorial to World War II Italian resistance fighters to find the narrow track leading to the Frescobaldi family's Castelgiocondo (www.frescobaldi.it). The modern, visitor-friendly winery produces "Lamaione", which became a must-have Merlot wine for late-1990s Hollywood celebs. Castelgiocondo's Sangiovese-based reds are atypically chocolatey for Brunello purists.

Next to Castelgiocondo are the vineyards of Luce della Vite (www.lucewines.com), whose internationally styled and very overpriced wines Frescobaldi co-produced with the Californian Mondavi family at Castelgiocondo until 2005.

Continue 3.2km (2 miles) through the woodland to the hamlet of Castiglion del Bosco (tel: 0577 807078; www.castigliondelbosco.com), whose castle-cum-winery of the same name produces reds for fairly early drinking under Massimo Ferragamo.

Then the road descends out of the woods, past a sign to the rather pedestrian, large-production Tenute Silvio Nardi (info@tenutenardi.com) on the left, into the valley where the Ombrone and Arbia rivers meet, and across fertile arable land. After 13km (8 miles) you reach the town of Buonconvento, whose ugly suburban housing gives way to some striking 14th-century city walls containing a thriving ex-pat British community.

Turn right onto the main road, the S2. This is also known as the "Via Cassia", the Roman road connecting Siena with Rome. From Buonconvento you can head towards the commune of Torrenieri 5km (3 miles) away, where the leading names are Innocenti (tel: 0577 834227) for light, early drinking Rosso di Montalcino; Casanova di Neri (www.casanovadineri.com) for a pleasant if clinical style of Sangiovese; and Podere La Vigna (tel: 0577 834252; www.poderelavigna.it) for Brunellos of classic weight.

The heart of Montalcino

However, our route takes us to Montalcino, whose fortified walls loom directly ahead, and above the Via Cassia. So after 2km (1.2 miles) on the S2 from Buonconvento turn right onto the SP45 for Montalcino. After 1.6km (1 mile) the visitor-friendly Altesino (tel: 0577 806131) and Tenuta Caparzo (tel: 0577 848390) are signposted on the left. Both are now under the same ownership, with Altesino known historically for fairly approachable reds, although these have been rather inconsistent lately, and Caparzo for both its single-vineyard Brunello "La Casa" and for a rich, slightly buttery, dry Chardonnay-based white "Le Grance". Both Altesino and Caparzo's most complex-tasting wines come from vineyards nearer the town around the hill of Montosoli, where the best vines of Montalcino's northern half are sited.

For the Montosoli vineyards, continue towards Montalcino on the SP45 for 4km (2.5 miles). On the way you will pass Fontepetri wine shop and Il Paradiso di Frassina (see p.105).

Near the technically adept winery of Valdicava (tel: 0577 848261) you will see, signposted on the right, a number of mainly small, family owned wineries. These include the Sassetti family's Pertimali (tel: 0577 848721), source of sometimes

LEFT Banfi castle was originally known as the Poggio alle Mura or "the walled hilltop".

WINERIES IN MONTALCINO

PRICES: moderate to expensive

Brunelli [B2]
Loc Martoccia
53024 Montalcino (SI)
Tel: 0577 848540
brunelli@cheapnet.it

Campi di Fonterenza [D3]
Podere Fonterenza, 99
Loc Sant'Angelo in Colle
53024 Montalcino (SI)
Tel: 0577 844248

Capanna di Cencioni [B1]
Loc Capanna, 333
53024 Montalcino (SI)
Tel: 0577 848298

Castello Banfi [D2]
Castello di Poggio alle Mura
Loc Sant'Angelo Scalo
53024 Montalcino (SI)
Tel: 0577 840111
CBMail@banfi.com
www.castellobanfi.com

Ciacci Piccolomini d'Aragona [D4]
Via Borgo di Mezzo, 62
Fraz Castelnuovo Abate
53024 Montalcino (SI)
Tel: 0557.835616
info@ciaccipiccolomini.com
www.ciaccipiccolomini.com

Donatella Cinelli Colombini [B1] Fattoria del Casato
Loc Casato Prime Donne
53024 Montalcino (SI)
Tel: 0577 849421
vino@cinellicolombini.it
www.cinellicolombini.it

Fattoria dei Barbi [B2]
Loc Podernovi, 170
53024 Montalcino (SI)
Tel: 0577 841111
info@fattoriadeibarbi.it
www.fattoriadeibarbi.it

ABOVE AND RIGHT *Typical Tuscan scenery – filled with history.*

WHERE TO BUY WINE

Enoteca Bruno Dalmazio [B3]
Via Trav dei Monti, 214
53024 Montalcino (SI)
Tel: 0577 849019
info@brunodalmazio.it
www.brunodalmazio.it or
www.dalmazio.com
Bruno Dalmazio's well-laid-out wine store has a massive selection of Brunello, plus wines from other Italian regions and oil, pasta, and wine accessories. Can ship worldwide. Free parking.

Enoteca Frantoio La Spiga [B3]
Via Circonvallazione, 212
53024 Montalcino (SI)
Tel: 0577 848611
Montalcino's olive oil cooperative was founded in the 1950s. Its shop on the ring road just below Montalcino's fortress offers direct sale of olive oil, Montalcino wine, and guided tours of the (modern) olive press. Free parking. Closed Thursday.

heady reds; Benito Cencioni's Capanna (*see* p.107), where soft, tangily sweet Moscadello whites complement tight-grained Brunello reds that open out well after several years in bottle and decanting; the historically renowned, but rather inconsistent, Barricci family's Podere Colombaio di Montosoli (tel: 0577 848599); Casanuova delle Cerbaie (tel: 0577 849284), whose reds are far cleaner and better constructed than its near-neighbour and near-namesake Cerbaia; La Mannella (www.lamannella.it) and Fastelli (tel: 0577 84825), who produce light reds; Le Chiuse and Gianni Brunelli who opt for reds tasting of older wood and dried fruit; Tenuta La Torracia, whose reds are atypically rich and soft; and Donatella Cinelli Colombini (*see* p.107). This estate, called Il Casato, was a hunting lodge (and honeymoon house) and has been in the same family since the 16th century, passing through the female line, a fact commemorated by "Le Prime Donne", a coffee-scented Brunello di Montalcino from the estate's best vines. Visitors can see an exhibition outlining the history and origins of Montalcino. Dry white wines and reds are also made from the new Orcia denomination, of which Donatella Cinelli Colombini was a founder (*see* p.117).

Oak ageing
Continue on the SP45, passing the Tenimenti Angelini's huge Val di Suga (tel: 0577 80411) winery on the left, for one of Montalcino's most outspoken winemakers, Giancarlo Pacenti of Sirò Pacenti (*see* p.111). The Brunellos here are aged in small oak barrels, and not larger wooden vats, so their creamy oak sheen either enhances the Brunello grape's rougher edges or destroys Brunello's typicity – depending on your point of view.

On the right-hand side, a warren of unsurfaced roads leads to several wineries of note around the Montosoli hill, including: Lambardi, whose old-style wines smell of cedar and the forest floor; La Gerla (tel: 0577 848599), whose modern-style reds agreeably balance Sangiovese's red fruit with oak flavour, and with the "Birba" bottling, Bordeaux grapes like Cabernet, too; the Guerrini family's Il Paradiso di Manfredi (*see* p.106), which produces less than 10,000 bottles of Rosso and Brunello combined, but it is a case of small is beautiful, such is the clarity, texture, and stylishness of both fruit and tannin, testament to the energy and refinement that can originate from the Montosoli slopes; Sante Marie (tel: 0577 847081; www.santemarie.it), which has recently opted for an international style of Brunello, with youthful grapes and well-judged use of new French oak.

A little further on along the SP45, on the left-hand side, Fuligni (*see* p.106) is signposted and offers more classic wines than those of Sirò Pacenti (and good olive oil, too), with lovely fruit rather than oak flavours to the fore. To visit the cavernous cellars under a 15th-century palace in Montalcino you must call well ahead. Fuligni's wines age in large wooden ovals (*botti*) rather than small French barriques.

Carry on to the roundabout, ignoring signs left to Torrenieri, and bear towards Montalcino. The town where you started this route is a further 2.7km (1.7 miles) up the hill. On the way you pass the headquarters of Marco Tempori's Pian di Macina (tel: 0577 849035), a small but excellent producer of pure, typical Sangioveses grown in the southwest of Montalcino.

Keep heading up the hill, looking out for a couple of places where you can stop and admire the view, just before the Enoteca Bruno Dalmazio (*see* box, left) on a hairpin bend.

Route Two: Montalcino south

From the roundabout by Montalcino's *fortezza* follow the sign to Castelnuovo dell'Abate, passing Pian dell'Orino, source of harmonious, crisp Brunello, on the left (www.piandellorino.it).

Almost immediately after the road straightens Biondi-Santi (www.biondisanti.it) appears on the right, home to the family celebrated for creating Brunello di Montalcino in 1888. But avoid it if you feel that Biondi-Santi's wines are caught in that uneasy void between traditional Brunello showing the negative effects of older wood and the modern style with atypically soft fruit for Sangiovese grown on rocky terrain.

Better to continue 2.6km (1.6 miles), passing the simple red wines of Crocedimezzo (www.lacrociona.com), the pithily dry efforts of Scopone (www.winescopone.com), and La Lecciaia

WINERY RESTAURANTS

Castello di Camigliano [C2]
Loc Camigliano
Via d'Ingresso, 2
53024 Montalcino (SI)
Tel: 0577 844068
Traditional Tuscan cooking and generous portions in medieval surroundings.

Le Potazzine [B3]
Piazza Garibaldi, 8/11
53024 Montalcino (SI)
Tel: 0577 849418
Centrally located, offering stylish food and efficient service. Popular with locals.

Ristorante Banfi [D3]
Costa Castellare, 1/3
53020 Sant'Angelo in Colle (SI)
Tel: 0577 816054
Michelin-starred cooking plus impressive wines. Expensive.

Ristorante Taverna dei Barbi
Loc Podernovi, 170
53024 Montalcino (SI)
Tel: 0557 847117
Homely restaurant serving home-produced *salumi* and *pecorino* cheese. Book ahead.

WINERIES IN MONTALCINO

PRICES: moderate to expensive

Azienda Agraria Lisini [D3]
Loc Sant'Angelo in Colle
53024 Montalcino
Tel: 0577 864040

Mastrojanni [D4]
Loc San Pio e Loreto
Fraz Castelnuovo dell'Abate
53024 Montalcino (SI)
Tel: 0577 835681
mastrojanni.vini@
mastrojanni.com
www.mastrojanni.com

Poggio San Polo [C4]
Loc Podere San Polo, 161
53024 Montalcino (SI)
Tel: 0577 835522
sanpolo@tetinet.com

Poggio di Sotto [D4]
Fraz Castelnuovo dell'Abate
Loc Poggio di Sopra, 222
53024 Montalcino (SI)
Tel: 0577 835502
palmuccipds@libero.it

Salicutti [C4]
Loc Podere Salicutti, 174
53024 Montalcino (SI)
Tel: 0577 847003
leanza@poderesalicutti.it
www.poderesalicutti.it

San Giuseppe [D4]
Loc San Giuseppe
53020 Castelnuovo
dell'Abate (SI)
Tel: 0577 835754
stella.violadicampalto@tin.it

San Lucia [B2]
Loc San Lucia
53024 Montalcino (SI)
Tel: 0577 847156
walterpierangioli@virgilio.it

Sesti [D2]
Castello di Argiano
Fraz Sant'Angelo in Colle
53024 Montalcino (SI)
Tel: 0577 843921

(www.lecciaia.it) for signs on the left-hand side and up a small track to Fattoria dei Barbi (see p.107).

Owned by the Cinelli Colombini family (see Donatella Cinelli Colombini in Montalcino Route One), Fattoria dei Barbi boasts the airy and enlightening museum, the Museo della Comunità di Montalcino e del Brunello (map ref C3; tel: 0577 846098; www.museodelbrunello.it).

Opened in April 2005, the museum contains old agricultural machinery, vineyard and winery equipment, working clothes and costumes used for traditional festivals, photographs, and audio-visual vignettes of traditional Montalcino crafts like the tanning of leather for shoemaking (the local cork oaks being the source of the tannin). There are also drawings showing how the area planted to vines in the Montalcino region has changed, with the most recent expansion of plantings in the south. These images also show, as owner Stefano Cinelli Colombini says, how Montalcino is shaped like a half-moon. The Barbi wine range is big, with good value IGT reds and older vintages of its long-lived and classically styled Brunellos for sale, some of which come from vines planted before World War II. They are said to be the oldest in production in Montalcino.

Biodiversity in the vineyards

Carry on for Salicutti (see boxes, left and p.105). Salicutti's owner Francesco Leanza farms four small but beautiful vineyards divided by strips of forest and olive groves. Leanza shuns chemical sprays so his vineyards almost resemble gardens. IGT red wines like "Duemiladue" and "Dopoteatro" seamlessly combine the respectively red and black fruit flavours of Sangiovese and Cabernet Sauvignon. Salicutti's Brunellos are acknowledged by his peers as among the very best that Montalcino has to offer, with lively, textured, almost creamy fruit backed up by ripe, insistent tannins with an endlessly appealing, wild edge.

A little further on is Poggio San Polo (see box, left), where the Fertonani family produces fairly priced, approachable but agreeably complex Brunello and Rosso di Montalcino with plenty of soft, wild fruit flavour and a hint of blackcurrant. Adjacent to this is the up-and-coming, pesticide-free Poggio San Polino (see p.105), whose red wines show bold flavours of new oak barrels. Back on the main road continue past La Poderina (tel: 0577 835737), which makes a good late-harvested Moscadello showing dried fig aromas in the best years, plus bright Brunellos made in a juicy modern style; La Fiorita, whose wines age rather rapidly; and Poggio Il Castellare (tel: 0577 940600) whose reds are rather medicinal.

After 4.5km (2.8 miles) you reach Castelnuovo dell'Abate and its remarkable abbey, the Abbazia di Sant'Antimo (map ref D4). There is a souvenir and book shop on the approach road

(with restrooms). The abbey was founded in the 9th century and is one of the finest examples of Romanesque architecture in Italy. It is open daily, and services sung to the Gregorian chant by Augustinian monks are open to the public.

Wineries in or around the centre of the town include Fanti (www.fantisanfilippo.com), source of chocolatey Brunellos that can flatter to deceive; La Colombina (www.lacolombinavini.it), which looks for a crisp, early-picked style for its green-tasting reds; and San Giorgio, which opts for the supermarket style of red, memorable only for its cheap price.

Up the hill, on an unsurfaced road from Castelnuovo dell'Abate is Mastrojanni (*see* box, left). Castelnuovo dell'Abate is one of the warmest sub-zones of Montalcino, but is high enough to get cooling breezes in summer. Mastrojanni's best Brunello is from the Vigna Schiena d'Asino, or "donkey's back" vineyard after the shape of the hillock on which the vines grow. There is also an intense, honeyed, late-picked white from nobly-rotten and sun-dried Malvasia, Moscato, Riesling, and Chardonnay grapes called "San Pio Botrys".

Enjoy the view

Admire the great views of Monte Amiata, then back down in Castelnuovo dell'Abate follow signs on the S323 to Seggiano and Stazione Monte Amiata for Poggio di Sotto (*see* box, left). Owners Elisabeth and Piero Palmucci produce warming, rich, chocolatey reds from a mix of old and young vines, using modern stainless-steel tanks and traditional Slovenian oak vats.

ABOVE *A beautiful sunset over Montalcino.*

WINERIES IN MONTALCINO

PRICES: moderate to expensive

Sirò Pacenti [B1]
Loc Pelagrilli, 1
53024 Montalcino (SI)
Tel: 0577 848662
pacentisiro@libero.it

Tenuta di Argiano [D2]
Loc Sant'Angelo in Colle, 74
53024 Montalcino (SI)
Tel: 0577 844037
argiano@argiano.net
www.argiano.net

Tenuta Corte Pavone [B2]
Loc Casanuova
53024 Montalcino (SI)
Tel: 0577 848110
www.loacker.net

La Torre [B2]
Loc La Torre
53020 Sant'Angelo in Colle (SI)
Tel: 0577 844073
luigi.anania@libero.it

ABOVE *Sesti's 13th century tower guards Montalcino.*

CAFFÈS AND PIZZERIAS

Caffè Bar Le Logge [B3]
Via Matteotti, 1
53024 Montalcino (SI)
Tel: 0577 846186
winebar.lelogge@email.it
Good selection of wines – off the Piazza del Popolo.

Kaffeina [B3]
Via Soccorso Saloni, 35
53024 Montalcino (SI)
Tel: 0577 849408
www.kaffeina.org
Wine bar offering hot and cold snacks and live music. Popular with young crowd.

Ristorante Pizzeria Il Marrucheto [D2]
Via della Stazione, 7
Sant'Angelo Scalo
53024 Montalcino (SI)
Tel: 0577 808000
Popular haunt for locals and tourists. Closed Thursday.

A bit further on, on the opposite side of the road, is San Giuseppe (*see* p.110) where Stella Viola di Campalto produces fantastic olive oil from trees planted in the 1920s, plus around 11,000 bottles of moreish Sangiovese-based red wines from young vines using a gravity-fed, underground cellar.

Other wineries here include Palagetto (www.palagetto.it), Tenuta Oliveto, and Anfora D'Oro, all sources of old-fashioned red wines, plus the more modern but soulless La Velona (www.lavelona.com), whose reds have more colour than flavour.

To go skiing continue on this road to Stazione Monte Amiata. The old volcano in the heart of the Apennines is the highest peak in Tuscany, south of the Arno River (1,738 metres/5,649 feet). You can also get here via the town of Abbadia San Salvatore.

Medieval cellars

Back in the centre of Castelnuovo dell'Abate follow signs from near the abbey to Sant'Angelo in Colle. After less than 1.6km (1 mile) the road becomes unsurfaced and on the right is Ciacci Piccolomini d'Aragona (*see* p.107). The Ciacci Piccolomini family produced Pope Pius II but died out in 1985, so the estate was inherited by the then manager, Giuseppe Bianchini, and his family. Atmospheric, medieval underground cellars belie very modern-style reds aged in new French oak barrels, such as the Cabernet Sauvignon and Sangiovese "Ateo", meaning "atheist". Its name is not a reflection of any ill-feeling toward this estate's Papal ancestry, more an expression of how French grapes like Cabernet Sauvignon can enhance the near-sacred Montalcino staple, the Brunello. Ciacci Piccolomini d'Aragona also offers accommodation (tel: 0577 835668) and has its own restaurant, Ristorante Le Ferraiole (tel: 0577 835796).

Continue for 2.7km (1.7 miles), passing Uccelliera (www.uccelliera-montalcino.it), whose clean, mouth-wateringly elegant reds provide a lively accompaniment to dinner; Le Presi (www.lepresi.it), which combines plump Sangiovese fruit with the taste of older wood; Tenuta di Sesta, whose reds are thick and sticky; Collosorbo (www.collosorbo.com) for appealing crisp reds for early drinking; and Sesta di Sopra (tel: 0577 835698), where the reds are soft and generously weighted.

Stop at Azienda Agraria Lisini (see p.110). Here the wines soften in large old chestnut vats rather than smaller, newer oak barrels to avoid masking the fruit with oak flavours. The vineyards command a great (and strategic) view over the Orcia Valley, as a look-out tower dating from 1300 testifies. Lorenzo Lisini Baldi's best plot, Ugolaia, produces mouth-filling Brunello di Montalcino from old vines on sun-drenched, south-facing slopes. Lisini provides one of the best examples of how different Brunello di Montalcino and Rosso di Montalcino should taste: the former dense and compact like fruit in Tuscan *panforte*, the latter softer and juicier, like English Christmas cake.

Continue for 2.7km (1.7 miles) for La Torre (see p.111), where cedar-scented reds reminiscent of classic old Bordeaux clarets are made. Oenologist Luigi Anania planted vines here in 1976 after finishing studies in agrarian science, including a thesis on the differences produced in the wines of Brunello according to vineyard location. He then selected this part of the southern Montalcino zone because of the slightly warmer climate: "the Sicily of Montalcino" he calls it. The wines soften in Slovenian oak casks and carry pure, mineral-driven flavours.

A short diversion

At the T-junction with the Montalcino–Grosseto road (the SP14) turn right to head back to Montalcino. On the way you'll find Poggio Antico, a winery and restaurant with good views and a seasonal menu (tel: 0577 849200; www.poggioantico.com); Villa a Tolli (tel: 0577 848498), whose Brunellos exude blackcurrant aromas with French oak; Casisano Colombaio (www.brunello.org), producing rich, leathery Brunellos; Piombaia (see p.105); and Ventolaio (tel: 0577 835779), whose light reds need decanting to dispel the varnishy note.

Our route, however, turns left onto he Montalcino–Grosseto road (the SP14) and left again after 1.6km (1 mile) to the tiny hilltop village of Sant'Angelo in Colle. This has commanding views south towards the Montecucco region (see pp.134–6).

WHERE TO BUY WINE

Caffè 1888 Fiaschetteria [B3]
Antica Cantina del Brunello
Piazza del Popolo, 6
53024 Montalcino (SI)
Tel: 0577 849043
fiaschetteria.italiana@tin.it
Famous, centrally located *caffè* founded in 1888 by Ferruccio Biondi-Santi, who created Brunello. The wine shop offers tastings (book ahead) and can arrange winery visits. Closed Thursday in winter.

Enoteca Bacchus [B3]
Via Giacomo Matteotti, 15
53024 Montalcino (SI)
Tel: 0577 847054
enotecabacchusmontalcino@yahoo.it
Wine plus Pienza *pecorino* cheese, cold meats (boar and deer), extra virgin olive oil, and honey.

Enoteca La Fortezza di Montalcino [B3]
Piazzale Fortezza
53024 Montalcino (SI)
Tel: 0577 829211
fortezza@enotecalafortezza.it
www.enotecalafortezza.it
Wine shop in Montalcino's fortress offering wine tastings and cold meats, cheeses, olive oil, and honey.

Enoteca Grotta di Brunello [B3]
Costa di Piazza Garibaldi, 3
53024 Montalcino (SI)
Tel: 0577 848095
grottadelbrunello@tin.it
An old wine cellar with a room dedicated to Brunello grappa. Honey, pasta, oil, and jam, too.

Enoteca di Piazza [B3]
Piazza Garibaldi, 4
53024 Montalcino (SI)
Tel: 0577 849194
Good service and wide selection of Super Tuscans. Wine tastings by prior appointment. English spoken.

WHERE TO EAT

**Ristorante Boccon
di Vino [B3]**
Loc Colombaio Tozzi, 201
53024 Montalcino (SI)
Tel: 0577 848233
The name translates as "a
slug of wine". Try *peposo*
(beef doused in pepper),
tortellini with saffron and
truffles or *carrabaccia* (onion
soup with *pecorino* cheese).

**Ristorante Grappolo Blu
[B3]** Scale di Via Moglio, 1
53024 Montalcino (SI)
Tel: 0577 847150
www.grappoloblu.it
One of the biggest wine
lists in Montalcino. Try
rabbit stewed in Brunello or
ravioli with local *pecorino*.

Osteria d'Altri Tempi [B3]
Vicolo Landi, 1
53024 Montalcino (SI)
Tel: 0577 846087
Big menu mixing traditional
dishes with modern. Good
selection of Pienza cheeses.

Trattoria Il Pozzo [D3]
53020 Sant'Angelo in
Colle (SI)
Tel: 0577 844015
Closed Tuesday. Quiet
restaurant with traditional
Tuscan cooking such as
bread soup (ask for it
without the bread), rabbit
with onions, and fruit pies.

Here you'll find a number of estates, including Collemattoni (www.collemattoni.it), where the fruit-driven, modern reds are light but well executed; Campogiovanni, whose Brunellos are user-friendly in terms of their ultra-open texture, but atypical of the zone; and Talenti (tel: 0577 844064; www.talentimontalcino.it), an estate created when the late winemaker Pierluigi Talenti was given vines at Pian di Conte by his employers, Il Poggione, after decades of service there. Pierluigi's grandson Riccardo now produces smooth reds aged in barrels in an impressive underground cellar, and very peppery stone-pressed olive oil.

Il Poggione (*see* p.106), on the right as you enter Sant'Angelo in Colle, is one of the few Montalcino vineyards to produce its own extra virgin olive oil on site. It also makes Moscadello, here in sparkling form. The best wines are reds like the open-textured Brunello di Montalcino *riserva* from the Paganelli vineyard. The vines were planted in the 1960s.

Dividing the inheritance

Il Poggione was created in 1958 when the Franceschi family divided their land. Roughly half (600 hectares) became Il Poggione, while the rest became the 550-hectare Col d'Orcia (www.coldorcia.it). This estate is reached by turning left out of Sant'Angelo in Colle, and continuing 8km (5 miles) to Sant'Angelo Scalo, where Col d'Orcia is signposted.

On the way you pass the headquarters of Campi di Fonterenza (*see* p.107), run by the twin Capadovani sisters. They make a generously thick style of Rosso di Montalcino from organic vineyards located near those of Salicutti (*see* p.110). They make powerful organic olive oil, too.

Sant'Angelo Scalo is nondescript architecturally, but boasts one of Tuscany's finest butchers, Macelleria e Norcineria Carlo Pieri (tel: 0577 808006). It is more famous as the headquarters of the giant American-owned Castello Banfi and its Castello di Poggio alle Mura (*see* p.107). There are free cellar tours, but a small charge is made for tasting the modern, sometimes flavourless, range of wines and to visit Banfi's amazing Museum of Glass and Wine (open daily; map ref D3). This traces the history of glass, with pieces by Dali and Picasso, and has the world's largest collection of unbroken Roman glassware. There is also a restaurant (*see* p.109) and a vinegar cellar.

Cosmic wine

Head back towards Montalcino and turn left after 4.8km (3 miles) up a forested dirt track for Tenuta di Argiano and Sesti (*see* p.110). The Sesti family's vines and olive trees are overlooked by the ruined 13th-century Castello di Argiano, and they are worked according to lunar cycles. Owner Giuseppe Sesti used to write cosmic calendars, having studied ancient astronomy in

Morocco in the 1960s. Brunello and Rosso di Montalcino with wild fruit flavours, plus the invitingly ripe "Terra di Sesti", a Cabernet/Merlot blend, are consistently good quality.

A little further on up the hill from Sesti on the dirt track is Tenuta di Argiano (see pp.105 and 111). Under the huge 16th-century villa are barrel-filled caverns where pure-tasting Brunello and Rosso di Montalcino, plus stylish reds like the 100% Sangiovese "Suolo" (the soil) and the Cabernet, Merlot, and Syrah blend called "Solengo" (lone wild boar) are aged.

Turn left from Argiano on a dirt track through olive groves, cereal crops, and vineyards for 3.2km (2 miles), direction Tavernelle, for Fossacolle (see p.106), where refreshingly clean Rosso and Brunello di Montalcino reds are made.

At the junction at the end of Fossacolle's drive you can turn left towards Camigliano. This hamlet surrounds its 14th-century church and the Castello di Camigliano (see p.109). The wines have improved recently, notably the top "Gualto Selezione" Brunello di Montalcino, in a peppery style, and the fruit-pastille-like Cabernet Sauvignon (Sant'Antimo Rosso). At Camigliano each September the Feast of the Rooster (La Sagra del Galletto) sees hundreds of chickens roasted over open coals.

Other wineries around Camigliano include Cupano (tel: 0577 816055; www.cupano.it), a source of light but elegant reds made by French cinematographer Lionel Cousin, who planted vineyards on land that had been abandoned, and Collelceto (tel: 0577 816022), whose clean Brunellos mix chocolate and blackberry fruit.

Wineries in Tavernelle

To get back to Montalcino from Fossacolle turn right, passing through Tavernelle. Here you'll find Roberto Bellini's Podere Brizio (tel: 0577 847154) and the estate he sold to famed Piemontese winemaker Angelo Gaja, the Pieve di Santa Restituta (not open to visitors). Bellini seems to have kept the best portions of vineyards from Gaja's clutches, and although his wines are expensive, they offer far better value for money, and more soul, than the more manicured wines of Gaja.

Also in Tavernelle is Case Basse, a meticulously farmed vineyard producing powerful but ethereal Brunellos, and Caprili (www.caprili.it), producing spritzy Moscadello white and delicate, cherry-scented Brunello. It is then a short drive up the hill to the T-junction where you follow signs back to Montalcino.

LEFT *The Tuscan countryside is home to a wealth of flowering plants and shrubs.*

BELOW *The vines just starting to burst their buds in spring.*

Montepulciano and the Orcia Valley

As Montalcino's great rival for reds made only from the Sangiovese grape, the elegant hilltop and more roomy town of Montepulciano (compared to Montalcino) suffers something of an inferiority complex. Just as they don't call Sangiovese by its real name in Montalcino, using the moniker Brunello instead, so in Montepulciano Sangiovese becomes Prugnolo Gentile, the "soft dark brown one".

Wine for the nobles

Soft and dark brown is a good description of Montepulciano's red wines. The sandy soils here make for soft fruit textures and wines that age relatively quickly, turning from ruby red to warm orange and garnet within two to five years of the harvest. One advantage of this is that they are more approachable – and often better value – than Brunello di Montalcino; but only a select few have Brunello's class (*see* wineries to visit).

Don't be put off by the term "Vino Nobile di Montepulciano" or "the noble wine of Montepulciano". Local wine-growers – called "*Poliziani*" after the town's most famous son, the poet and classical scholar Angelo Ambrogini or Il Poliziano – are not snobs, they just use the term because their wines were historically drunk by the nobility. So, think of the term as meaning "wine for the nobles" rather than a "noble wine" per se.

The real confusion comes because Montepulciano is also the name of a red grape from the Abruzzo called Montepulciano d'Abruzzo, but plantings of that in Tuscany are mainly confined to Grosseto province.

Good value drinking

If you are on a tight budget, ignore Vino Nobile di Montepulciano or *riserva* in favour of Montepulciano Rosso, a red wine that has had minimal ageing. These are the ones to go for during an impromptu picnic, as their fresh fruit needs immediate drinking.

In Montepulciano the main event of the year is the Bravìo delle Botti, a barrel rolling competition between the town's eight wards (*contrade*). The barrels used to be rolled full of wine and although they are now empty, they still weigh 80kg (177 pounds). The Bravìo takes place on the last Sunday in August and is preceded by 10 days of sweat-inducing festivities and feasting.

Tuscany's top truffles

The two main wine regions either side of Montepulciano are Cortona and more significantly the Orcia Valley, where Sangiovese-based reds dominate. In wine terms the Orcia Valley is something of a Cinderella, sandwiched between two elder sisters of Montalcino and Montepulciano. This is a beautiful area of cereal farms and sheep grazing, the milk being used for cheese-making, for which Pienza is the main production area. Olive oil is a big part of the local economy, too, and the local truffles are said to be Tuscany's finest (see the truffle fairs of San Giovanni d'Asso, p.121).

Getting there

The easiest railway station is not the infrequently served Montepulciano Stazione but Chianciano-Terme, on the Rome–Florence line. A daily bus service from Siena, via Pienza, is operated by TRAIN. Drive to Montepulciano via Pienza from Siena or Montalcino, or take the Chianciano Terme exit off the A1 Rome–Florence motorway. Non-residents are banned from driving in Montepulciano's town centre.

Travelling around

Route summary This route goes in a circle from Buonconvento to Torrenieri, San Quirico d'Orcia, Ripa d'Orcia, Pienza, Montepulciano, Montepulciano Stazione, Torrita di Siena, Montisi, San Giovanni d'Asso, and back to Buonconvento. The route length is 150–220km (94–137 miles). Allow two to three days.

Route: Montepulciano and Orcia Valley

From Buonconvento take the Via Cassia south, direction Rome, and go to Torrenieri for Podernuovo (see p.120). It lies on the Torrenieri–San Giovanni d'Asso road (left-hand side, before La Canonica). Podernuovo is run by one of the Orcia Valley's most talented winemakers, Federico Bartolomei. Bitingly clear Orcia Rossos with generous flavour are made, like the 100% Sangiovese "Nectar" and the "Podernuovo", which has a bit of Syrah and Cabernet blended in. Next door is a very good cheese producer called Vergelle – Caseificio.

From Torrenieri head southeast to San Quirico d'Orcia where, at Via Dante, 96, you'll find the winery of Sampieri del Fa'Brogi (tel: 0577 897543, www.collinedivignoni. toscana.nu). Solid reds aged in a mix of cement and chestnut vats are made, with the estate's olive oil kept in amphorae in the winery annexe. Sampieri del Fa'Brogi's vines are found around the elevated fortified medieval hamlet of Vignoni just outside San Quirico d'Orcia, together with three agritourism apartments for rental.

WINERIES IN MONTEPULCIANO

Boscarelli [B4]
Fraz Cervognano
Via di Montenero, 28
53040 Montepulciano (SI)
Tel: 0578 767277
www.poderiboscarelli.com

Dei [B4]
Loc Villa Martiena, 35
53045 Montepulciano (SI)
Tel: 0578 716878
info@cantinedei.com
www.cantinedei.com

Massimo Romeo [C4]
Fraz Gracciano di
Montepulciano
Loc Nottola
Podere Corsica, 25
53045 Montepulciano (SI)
Tel: 0578 708599

Podere le Bèrne [B4]
Fraz Cervognano
Via Poggio Golo, 7
53040 Montepulciano (SI)
Tel: 0578 767328
leberne@libero.it
www.leberne.it

Poliziano [C4]
Loc Montepulciano Stazione
Via Fontago, 1
53040 Montepulciano (SI)
Tel: 0578 738171
az.agpoliziano@iol.it

═══ Route: Montepulciano and Orcia Valley

Allow two to three days

▬ Montalcino

▬ Montepulciano and Val d'Orcia

0   5 Km
0   5 miles

Saffron renaissance

The Orcia Valley is currently regaining its reputation as a centre for saffron production, a skill that was lost after the Middle Ages. One of the best local producers of *zafferano* is Antonio Brandi (Vicolo del Vecchietta, 5, 53027 San Quirico d'Orcia; tel: 0577 897726; www.crocusbrandi.it; map ref B2). Brandi sells his saffron on the crocus flowers' pistils, rather than as a powder, which is unusual but ensures maximum freshness. The Greek god Hermes saw saffron as essential for re-awakening one's dormant sexual desire, although modern chefs are more prosaic, using it to aromatize wild game and other meats.

Stay in a fortress

From San Quirico d'Orcia take the road past the football stadium (*stadio*) to the thermal spa town of Bagno Vignoni, bearing right to the castle of Ripa d'Orcia (*see* p.120) on an unsurfaced road with great views to Monte Amiata. The castle overlooks the heart of the Orcia Valley, and dates from the 13th century. It has been in the same family since the 15th. The fortress is a great place to stay (*see* the website for details of agritourism), and Ripa d'Orcia produces firm Sangiovese-based reds and a refreshing, oak-fermented dry white "Le Piaggie" from Chardonnay and Vermentino.

Wrapped in a vine

Return to San Quirico d'Orcia the way you came, passing Poggio al Vento (*see* box, right) on your left, and Sante Marie di Vignoni (*see* p.120) on your right. The Generali family's house was once Church property, and their small cellar used to be a stable for the animals. A good-value range of Merlot-, Sangiovese-, and Cabernet-based reds is made. The top wine, "Sunto", is sold with a vine pruning wrapped around its neck.

Sheep's milk cheese

Continue to Pienza, the centre of the Orcia Valley's cheese made from ewes' (*pecorino*) milk. Many of the local farmers, like the Cugusis of Fattoria La Buca Nova (*see* box, left) have Sardinian origins. From Pienza take the main road towards Montepulciano. Just before the turning to Montichiello turn right for Thomas Wulf's organic Podere Lignano (*see* p.120; English spoken). Tasty red and dry white wines are made, plus olive oil, and the vineyards and olive trees are terraced with evocative dry stone walls for support.

Back on the Pienza–Montepulciano road turn right for the Capitoni family's Sedime (*see* p.120). Sedime means "a place where travellers stop". The Capitonis are cereal and olive farmers who planted a small vineyard out of curiosity, but their attention to detail has paid dividends, and a pause here will reward you with red Sangiovese-based wines of burgundian elegance.

A noble tourist trap

The next stop is Montepulciano, famous for its "Vino Nobile". In the town centre, and opposite the town hall, is the winery of Contucci (www.contucci.it), something of a tourist trap, as the 16th-century cellars, the creaking wooden vats, and the smart tour guides are more memorable than the wines.

Avignonesi, another famous name in Montepulciano, has a shop in the town at Via di Graciano nel Corso, 91, above its impressive underground cellars, but the headquarters, winery, and *vinsantaia* for its famous *vin santo*, are now on the road to Cortona past Valliano, at Le Capezzine (www.avignonesi.it). Avignonesi's reds have an earthy, southern feel, while the dry whites under the Cortona DOC label are modern, crisp, and tropical.

ABOVE *Ancient towns perch atop hills.*

WHERE TO STAY

Agricampeggio Il Casale [B3]
Loc Casale, 64
53026 Pienza (SI)
Tel: 0578 755109
podereilcasale@libero.it
Atmospheric, chaotic farm with campsite. English spoken.

Castelnuovo Tancredi [C1]
53024 Buonconvento (SI)
Tel: 0577 808256
Attractive farmhouses dotted around its wooded estate.

Hotel Il Marzocco [B4]
Piazza Savonarola, 18
53045 Montepulciano (SI)
Tel: 0578 757262
www.albergoilmarzocco.it
Elegantly decaying 16th-century palace turned into a hotel by the Feci family.

Poggio al Vento [A2]
Loc Poggio al Vento
53023 Castiglione d'Orcia (SI)
Tel: 0577 897384
www.poggioalvento.net
Five apartments overlooked by the Monte Amiata to the south.

WINERIES IN ORCIA VALLEY
. . . .
**Castello di Ripa
d'Orcia [A2]**
Loc Ripa d'Orcia
53023 Castiglione
d'Orcia (SI)
Tel: 0577 897376
info@castelloripadorcia.com
www.castelloripadorcia.com

Podere Lignano [B3]
SS146 (Km 1/33)
53026 Pienza (SI)
Tel: 0578 748005

Podernuovo [B1]
Loc Podernuovo, 64
53020 San Giovanni
d'Asso (SI)
Tel: 0577 834249

Sante Marie di Vignoni [A2]
Loc Vignoni Alto
53027 San Quirico
d'Orcia (SI)
Tel: 0577 898141

Sedime [B3]
Podere Sedime, 63
53026 Pienza (SI)
Tel: 0578 748346
capitoni.marco@libero.it

Modern or traditional?

If you head south from Montepulciano towards Sant'Albino, you will pass the ultra-modern, gravity-fed winery of Salcheto (tel: 0578 799031; www.salcheto.it). This is a good source of sexily soft, yet positively oaky reds such as the Vino Nobile "Salco".

A more traditional-style winery, Dei (see p.117), is found by taking the road to Cervognano from Montepulciano's St Agnese church. The grandfather of the current owner, Caterina Dei, bought the estate as a holiday home, and the first wines were made only in 1985. Dei's Sangiovese reds offer good value, as use of oak is kept to a minimum, allowing the fruit to shine unhindered. The "Sancta Catharina" red made from Cabernet, Sangiovese, Syrah, and Petit Verdot is oaked, but sensitively so.

Vines on a hillock

Further towards the hamlet of Cervognano is Podere le Bèrne (see p.117). The Natalini family has been making wine here since 1960, and the name of the estate is derived from an ancient Etruscan term meaning "hillock" – which is always a good sign for a vineyard, since hilly rather than flat ground affords the best drainage and exposure to the sun. Le Bèrne's Vino Nobile di Montepulciano has typical Sangiovese flavours of red fruit mixed with burnt earth.

Between Cervognano and Acquaviva is Boscarelli (see p.117; by prior appointment only), a source of beautifully soft Vino Nobile with bright, smooth tannins and a lovely aftertaste of mint and blackcurrant. The sharply defined hills here afford excellent vine-growing conditions, and owners Marchese Luca de Ferrari Corradi and Nicolò de Ferrari take full advantage.

From Acquaviva you can travel to Gracciano, passing one of this zone's most underrated growers, Massimo Romeo (see p.117). Romeo farms four small plots of vines as if they were private gardens, and writes beautifully descriptive back labels to his ample red wines, all of which are aged in older wood.

Consistently balanced

From Gracciano head towards Abbadia and Torrita di Siena, but not before a quick diversion towards Montepulciano Stazione for a visit to Montepulciano's most consistent producer, Poliziano (see p.117), with its distinctive pink winery. Owners the Carletti family are superb wine-growers; they make wine only from their own grapes, and produce reds with a fine balance between fruit, mineral flavours, and oak where used. If you can't make it to the winery, the wines

LEFT *Time often stands still in the Orcia Valley.*

BELOW, LEFT *The "botti" or large oval barrels used to age red wine.*

are available from Poliziano's wine shop (*enoteca*) located in Piazza Grande, Montepulciano, which is open from April to October.

From Poliziano, if you cross the A1 Rome–Florence motorway you will enter the vineyards of the Cortona region, where the best producer, Manzano, makes mouth-filling Syrah-based red wines, a grape that seems to have a great future in Tuscany.

Up, up, and away

Return to Buonconvento via Torrita di Siena, Montisi, and San Giovanni d'Asso. In Montisi you can take a balloon trip over the beautiful Orcia Valley (*see* www. ballooningintuscany.com; English spoken; map ref C3), with a Champagne breakfast (the wind speed is better here in the mornings than the afternoons).

San Giovanni d'Asso has its feet planted more firmly on the ground since it is famous for its truffles, both the white *crete senesi* truffle (available from October 1 to December 31) and the darker *tartufo marzuolo* (in season from January to April). The town hosts a truffle festival in early March and mid-November each year.

WHERE TO EAT

Giannetti Eraldo [C2]
Loc Lucignano, 29
53020 San Giovanni
d'Asso (SI)
Tel: 0577 803109
Food shop turned (tiny) wine bar offering salami, ham, and cheese of excellent provenance.

Latte di Luna
Via San Carlo, 24
52042 Cortona (AR)
Tel: 0578 748606
Pici pasta with duck sauce, suckling pig with garlic and rosemary, and soft homemade ice cream.

Le Logge del Vignola [B4]
Via delle Erbe, 6
53045 Montepulciano (SI)
Tel: 0578 717290
Reliable dish of the day plus huge salads with seasonal greens, tomato, basil, and pepperoni in summer.

Osteria Acquacheta [B4]
Via del Teatro, 22
53045 Montepulciano (SI)
Tel: 0578 717086
Winter soups, roast veal, chicken liver pâté, and mushroom pasta. Evenings only.

Pizzeria Ristorante La Compagnia [B2]
Via Romana, 27
53028 Torrenieri (SI)
Tel: 0577 834265
Good value pizzeria popular with locals with homemade *pici* pasta. Closed Wednesday.

The Etruscan coast

It would have been nigh on impossible to travel down the Tuscan coast or Maremma just 150 years ago. If you didn't get bitten to death by the mosquitoes you'd have sunk ceaselessly into the swampy marshland that existed here until the land was drained. For the modern generation this has meant easier access to the region's parkland and beaches, while creating the road and rail infrastructure to make the establishment of working vineyards a reality.

Tuscan coast by any other name

But you'd be foolish to think that the Tuscan coast – or the Etruscan coast as the region's wine producers would have us call it – revolves solely around its star attraction of Bolgheri, the hot amphitheatre of hills around the town of Castagneto Carducci made famous by Sassicaia, the Super Tuscan red wine created by Tenuta San Guido in the late 1960s.

This changed the face of Tuscan red wine forever by proving that Bordeaux-style red wines could not just be made here but could flourish, as Sassicaia swatted away Bordeaux's best wines in blind tastings the world over. Sassicaia's success has seen Bolgheri become one of Italy's most sought-after regions, with the number of modern and far from characterful wineries that have sprung up inversely proportional to the number of value-for-money wines being produced there.

In Bolgheri save your money for a trip to the local bird reserve, Il Rifugio Faunistico di Bolgheri (open October to April by prior appointment; tel: 0565 224361; map ref. E2), to see peregrine falcons, cranes, storks, tawny owls, badgers, and bee-eaters; or spend your time more profitably getting to know the Etruscan coast's lesser lights like Montescudaio slightly to the north. Here the Mediterranean heat is tempered in vineyards that face northwest, providing powerful wines of great elegance. Or try the wines of Val di Cornia to the south, a warmer zone where vines revel in the heat, especially around Suverto, a hilltop town whose steep hairpin bends and cactus-stuffed walls, palm trees, and sea views are wine's equivalent of the Hollywood hills. The iron-rich soils here give red wines of great colour and power.

Wine island

We should not forget Elba, whose red wines like Aleatico *passito* can be as imperious as Elba's most famous former resident, Napoleon Bonaparte. Their wildness and depth of fruit mean they should not be written off as tourist fodder, even if half-

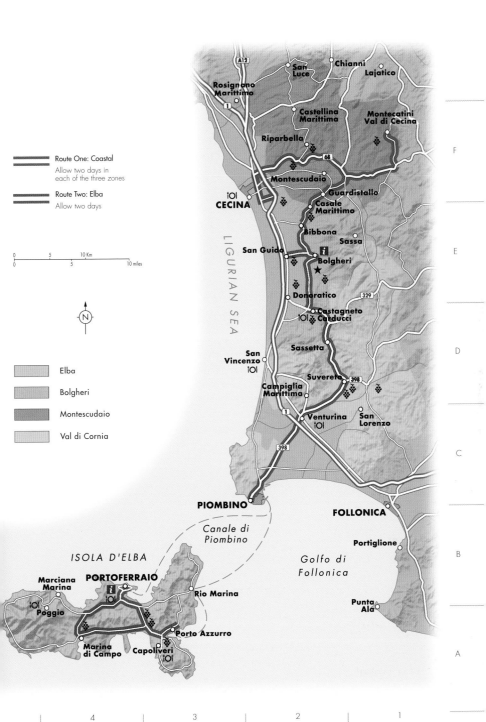

Route One: Coastal
Allow two days in
each of the three zones

Route Two: Elba
Allow two days

0   5   10 Km
0   5   10 miles

N

Elba

Bolgheri

Montescudaio

Val di Cornia

A12

San
Luce

Chianni

Lajatico

Rosignano
Marittimo

Castellina
Marittima

Montecatini
Val di Cecina

Riparbella

68

Montescudaio

Guardistallo

CECINA

Casale
Marittimo

LIGURIAN SEA

Bibbona

Sassa

San Guido

Bolgheri

Donoratico

329

Castagneto
Carducci

Sassetta

San
Vincenzo

Suvereto

398

D

Campiglia
Marittima

San
Lorenzo

1

Venturina

398

PIOMBINO

FOLLONICA

Canale di
Piombino

Portiglione

ISOLA D'ELBA

Golfo di
Follonica

Marciana
Marina

PORTOFERRAIO

Rio Marina

Punta
Ala

Poggio

Porto Azzurro

Marina
di Campo

Capoliveri

F

E

C

B

A

4

3

2

1

bottles of them often end up stuffed into rucksacks by day-trippers rushing for ferries to the mainland.

Getting there

The Etruscan coast is crossed by SS1 (Via Aurelia), which runs from Rome to Livorno. ATL run bus services in Livorno for Cecina, in Montescudaio, and ATM in Piombino for Val di Cornia and Castagneto Carducci in Bolgheri. There are regular rail services between Piombino (from Rome and Genoa) and Livorno (from Rome and Florence).

Travelling around

Route summaries There are two routes for the Etruscan coast. The first covers the mainland and the second covers the island of Elba.

Route One summary Our route for the Etruscan coast is shaped like the letter "T", beginning in Cecina in Montescudaio zone and running east to Montecatini Val di Cecina, then heading south via Guardistallo and Montescudaio and Bibbona to Bolgheri and Castagneto Carducci in the Bolgheri zone. Continue south in the Val di Cornia through Suvereto and Campiglia Marittima as far as Piombino, from where you catch the ferry to Elba. Allow a couple of days in each of the three zones (Montescudaio, Bolgheri, and Val di Cornia) covered.

Route Two summary The route for Elba follows the main road from Porto Azzurro to Portoferraio passing the hamlets of Mola, Gelsarello, and Acquabona, turning west towards Marciana Marina, turning south at Procchio for the airfield at La Pila, then heading east back to Porto Azzurro. Allow a couple of days from when you arrive on the island to enjoy Elba's beauty to the full.

Route One: Coastal

Find the SS68 Cecina–Volterra road, just to the north of Cecina itself and head in an easterly direction for about 8km (5 miles). If you follow the signs to the town of Riparbella, and from there carry on towards Castellina Marittima, you'll get to Carlo Paoli's

WHERE TO EAT IN MONTESCUDAIO

Enoteca Bibére [F2]
Via della Libertà
56040 Montescudaio (PI)
Tel: 0586 651951
Perfect match of grilled red meat and equally soft Montescudaio wines.

Enoteca Savio [E2]
Piazza Mazzini, 4
57020 Bibbona (LI)
Tel: 0586 671946
Eclectic range of wines by the glass and snacks to match. Open Easter to October.

Ristorante Il Becco Reale e Hotel Tornese [E2]
Viale Galliano, 36
57023 Cecina Mare (LI)
Tel: 0586 620703
Super sea front location and oven roasted sea bass are the main attractions here.

Trattoria Albana
Villaggio Mazzolla, 71
56048 Volterra (PI)
Tel: 0588 39001
Tiny family-run restaurant with generous steaks. Closed Tues.

Castello del Terriccio (tel: 0506 99709; www.terriccio.it), source of the Sangiovese "Capannino", which exudes blackberry flavours, and is a safer bet for medium-term ageing than the much lauded Bordeaux-style red "Lupicaia".

However, our route means that we stop before the town of Riparbella signposted on the left for La Regola (see box, right; by appointment). This is one of Montescudaio's most consistent wineries. The dry white "Steccaia" from Trebbiano, Vermentino, and Sauvignon Blanc is one of the best value-for-money white wines in the zone – a crisp, dry wine light enough to suit the seafood dishes of Cecina Mare's eateries to perfection. La Regola also produces a fuller-flavoured dry white, "Lauro", an enticing blend of nectarine-scented Viognier, creamy Chardonnay, and lightly exotic Sauvignon Blanc. La Regola's red wines are no less impressive. The Sangiovese-based "Beloro" is fermented with a yeast selected from vineyards in Montalcino, helping create a bitter black cherry finish beneath some wild and smoky oak flavours. "Ligustro" has a pinch of Colorino blended in with Sangiovese, but without oak, and shows immediately open textured fruit flavours. A more serious and concentrated red called "Cru La Regola" is a Bordeaux-style blend of Cabernet Sauvignon and Merlot.

French occupation

Carry on towards Volterra for Caiarossa (see box, right; by appointment), one of the most striking vineyards and wineries in Tuscany. The estate is owned by Château Giscours of Margaux in Bordeaux and, as in Bordeaux, the vineyards are planted at high density so that each vine is asked to bear only a relatively small number of grape bunches for extra concentration and elegance. Caiarossa's vineyards occupy an amphitheatre-like suntrap, which encourages late-ripening grapes like Cabernet Sauvignon, Petit Verdot, and Mourvèdre. The winery is built on several levels, using gravity from the moment the grapes arrive, through the fermentation process until ageing in barrel and bottling. There are also some wooden fermentation vats, to keep red wines at a constant temperature during and after fermentation for cleaner, more harmonious flavours. Caiarossa produces a solid range of reds including the generously weighted "La Serra" (Merlot and Petit Verdot), the wiry "La Botra" (a Cabernet-based blend), the crisp "La Sassa" (100% Sangiovese), and the exotic "La Ripa" (from Syrah, Grenache, Mourvèdre, and some of the white grape Viognier).

Continue on the Cecina–Volterra road as far as Montecatini Val di Cecina, where the landscape becomes more obviously hilly, rising to the zone's high of around 450 metres (1,476 feet), for Fattoria Sorbaiano (see box, right; by appointment). Owners the Piccolini family produce olive oil and cereal crops

WINERIES IN MONTESCUDAIO

Caiarossa [F2]
Loc Serra all'Olio, 59
56046 Riparbella (PI)
Tel: 0586 699016
www.caiarossa.it

Fattoria Sorbaiano [F2]
Loc Sorbaiano
56040 Montecatini
Val di Cecina (PI)
Tel: 0588 30243
www.fattoriasorbaiano.it

Pagani De Marchi Maria [E2]
Via della Camminata, 2
Loc La Nocera
56040 Casale Marittimo (PI)
Tel: 0586 653016
www.paganidemarchi.com

Poggio Gagliardo [E2]
Loc Poggio Gagliardo, 49
56040 Montescudaio (PI)
Tel: 0586 630661
www.poggiogagliardo.com

La Regola [F2]
Via A. Gramsci, 1
56046 Riparbella (PI)
Tel: 0586 698145
www.laregola.com

LEFT *Bolgheri's famous avenue.*

BELOW *Fresh lemons abound.*

BELOW *Sassicaia, home to the original Super Tuscan.*

as well as wine. Sorbaiano's eponymously named red from 80% Sangiovese and 10% each of Malvasia Nera and Montepulciano, is immediately appealing for its chocolate softness. Sorbaiano's "Rosso delle Miniere" ("miner's red"), whose name commemorates the Etruscans who first mined precious metals in this zone, sees Cabernet Franc replacing the Montepulciano, with the predictable result of the chocolate notes changing to violets and blackcurrants. One other winery of note in Montecatini Val di Cecina is Stefano Baldacci's L'Aione (tel: 0586 682698; by appointment). The Sangiovese-based red "Aione" is blended with 25% Cabernet Sauvignon and Cabernet Franc in a refreshingly subtle way; while the traditional Bordeaux blend "Etico" shows decent weight and density. There is obvious new oak, but rich black fruit on the palate with soft tannins; well constructed and very international.

Luncheon is served

From Sorbaiano head back toward the coast and Cecina on the Cecina–Volterra road, turning left (south) for Guardistallo and Casale Marittimo from where Poggio Gagliardo (*see* p.125) is signposted. If you book ahead the winery can serve lunch or dinner for up to 25 people, or a more simple buffet can be arranged. The signature white wine here is the "Vigna Lontana", which shows the kind of richness one would expect of a Chardonnay from the Mediterranean. The lighter-tasting "Linaglia" has Trebbiano for a more mouth-tingling feel and Viognier for apricot blossom flavour. Poggio Gagliardo's reds like "Gobo ai Pianacci" or "L'Ultimosole" are made in an approachable style, and show how Montescudaio reds combine firm flavours with soft textures. The Cabernet Franc vines here rank with those of Sassicaia's (*see* p.127) as the oldest along the Etruscan coast.

In Casale Marittimo you'll find Pagani De Marchi Maria (*see* p.125), home to a fine range of reds made in a juicy style, such as the typically leafy Merlot "Casa Nocera", the bitingly frank Sangiovese "Principe Guerriero", and blackcurrant- and apple-scented Cabernet "Casalvecchio".

From Casale Marittimo head to Bibbona, a hilltop town with tight, winding streets; this is soon to get its own region of origin denomination (DOC). Continue on to Bolgheri and Castagneto Carducci, around which the Bolgheri zone is delimited.

In with the in crowds

Bolgheri has become such a wine mecca that most wineries insist that you book ahead for a visit, especially during summer when the crowds here can become oppressive. However, during busy periods and without a reservation don't despair, as you may be able to tack yourself onto an existing tour if someone else has failed to show up. Failing that, go to Giovanni Chiappini's Podere Felciaino just south of Bolgheri (tel: 0565 749665; www.giovannichiappini.it) on the road to Castagneto Carducci, which is open daily with no prior reservation needed and whose red wines are fairly representative of Bolgheri but in a light, simple, fruity style. Before you get to Chiappini you pass the Ornellaia winery (www.ornellaia.it; visits by appointment and for groups only). This is built into the hillside rather like a secret bunker, with attractive gardens around and even on top of the winery roof, which is grassed. When Ornellaia first produced one of the original Super Tuscan reds, blending the Tuscan Sangiovese with Bordeaux grapes in the 1970s, it was a cutting edge winery; now it has become just another mainstream international-style wine, passing through a bewildering number of corporate owners in recent years.

The original Super Tuscan, however, is Sassicaia, from the Tenuta San Guido estate (see box, right; by prior appointment) encompassing the hamlet of Bolgheri. Owner Nicolò Incisa della Rocchetta's private house, the vineyards, and the surrounding scrub and prairies where he breeds champion racehorses are off-limits, but the visitor centre and winery are easily accessible by taking the road towards the coast from Bolgheri, along an avenue of cypresses almost 5km (3 miles) long, immortalized in a poem by Giouse Carducci that every Italian school child supposedly knows by heart. Sassicaia retains its classical appeal, despite the fame, with a Cabernet Sauvignon- and Cabernet Franc-dominated wine that is ripe without becoming jammy, and with an almost salty freshness to the tannins.

Near Sassicaia's cantina you'll find the superbly run tourist information centre (see p.122) which covers the whole of the Etruscan coast, the Consorzio Strada del Vino Costa degli Etruschi. They can help arrange visits – so call ahead before you leave for Italy so that you can visit the wineries you want, when you want to.

(see p.122)

WINERIES IN BOLGHERI

Grattamacco Collemassari [D2] Loc Grattamacco, 129
57022 Castagneto
Carducci (LI)
Tel: 0565 765069
www.grattamacco.com

Greppi Cupi [D2]
Loc Greppi Cupi, 212
57024 Castagneto
Carducci (LI)
Tel: 0565 775272
greppi.cupi@libero.it

Michele Satta [D2]
Loc Vigna al Cavaliere, 61
57022 Castagneto
Carducci (LI)
Tel: 0565 773041
satta@infol.it

Tenuta San Guido [E2]
Loc Capanne, 27
57020 Bolgheri (LI)
Tel: 0565 762003
www.sassicaia.com

WHERE TO EAT

Hotel Ristorante Zi' Martino [D2] Strada per Castagneto
Loc San Giusto, 264A
57022 Castagneto
Carducci (LI)
Tel: 0565 766000
Try the house pasta with mushrooms and wild rabbit.

Ristorante La Tana del Pirata [D2] Via Milano, 17
57024 Marina di
Castagneto Carducci (LI)
Tel: 0565 744143
Huge seafood selection. Closed Tuesday.

Ristorante Il Vecchio Frantoio [D2] Via Gramsci, 8,
57022 Castagneto,
Carducci (LI)
Tel: 0565 763731
Superb game, fish, and pizza.

Roll out the barrel

One of the best wineries to visit belongs to the modest Michele Satta (see p.127; by appointment), just south of Castagneto Carducci. Run by Michele and his wife Lucia, the tasting room has a homely feel, with much of the furniture made out of old wine barrels. Wooden fermentation vats are used for some of the red wines, which come from both Satta's own vines and rented plots to maximize blending opportunities. The Sattas' wines include "Cavaliere", one of Tuscany's purest-tasting Sangioveses, and the cleverly constructed "Piastraia", a four-way blend of Sangiovese, Merlot, Syrah, and Cabernet Sauvignon. The 100% Viognier "Giovin Re" shows plenty of rich fruit behind the vanilla tones from partial oak-barrel fermentation.

Wines with a more obviously international feel are made at Grattamacco (see p.127; groups only; by appointment). The name of the estate means "iron scraping", as the local stones had their iron ore extracted by the earliest settlers here, the Etruscans. The Grattamacco vineyards are some of the oldest in the Bolgheri zone, having been first planted in the 1940s, not long after the Sassicaia vineyards (see p.127). The owners, the Cavallari family, now rent them to the energetic businessman Claudio Tipa (of Colle Massari in Montecucco, see p.134), who has created a fantastic winery with earthen walls, stained glass, wooden fermentation vats for red wines, a barrel cellar for white wines, and great views for visitors. Grattamacco's dry white wine made from 100% Vermentino has perfectly weighted oak, with just 25% barrel-fermented, giving it the body to stand up to a hefty fish main course with a creamy sauce. Grattamacco's top red, a Bolgheri Superiore, from a blend of Merlot, Sangiovese, and Cabernet Sauvignon, is as vigorous and characterful as its maker.

Star-gazing and yoga

From Castagneto Carducci head south via Sassetta into the Val di Cornia zone and the town of Suvereto, which has its own sub-zone within the Val di Cornia. The leading winery here is Bulichella (*see* boxes, left and right; open daily), an organic farm and vineyard with a well-stocked farm shop (stone-milled olive oil, jam and marmalade, vegetables, and sauces) and which also runs well-being events which include Japanese massage and yoga, origami, and astronomy. Bulichella's red and white wines are easily among the best in Val di Cornia too, with smooth but pinpoint fruit flavours, delicious concentration, and a touch of minerality for complexity, too.

Another Suvereto winery with a good reputation is Nico Rossi and Maria Teresa Cabella's Gualdo del Re (*see* box, right; open daily), source of an impressively large range of wines including the intriguing dry white "Valentina" from Vermentino grapes, "Strale" from Pinot Bianco, and the Suvereto Sangiovese, which sees enough oak to round out its concentrated, jammy flavours. Similarly jammy or prune-like reds are available at the rapidly improving Incontri (tel: 0565 829401; open daily) but head to Montepeloso (*see* box, right) for reds with a bit more depth and finesse. Montepeloso's owner is the multi-lingual, jazz-loving Swiss-Italian Fabio Chiarelotto, a

WINERIES IN VAL DI CORNIA

Bulichella [C1]
Loc Bulichella 31
57028 Suvereto (LI)
Tel: 0565 829892
www.bulichella.it

Gualdo del Re [C1]
Loc Notri, 77
57028 Suvereto (LI)
Tel: 0565 829888
www.gualdodelre.it

Montepeloso [C1]
Loc Montepeloso, 82
57028 Suvereto (LI)
Tel: 0565 828180
contact@montepeloso.it

BELOW *Olive trees and vines share the land.*

meticulous grape-grower and winemaker. His varietal reds from Syrah and Sangiovese, and "Gabbro" Cabernet Sauvignon, are concentrated but not overextracted, while the Sangiovese, Montepulciano, and Cabernet Sauvignon blend "Nardo" evolves beautifully in the glass.

From Suvereto head southwest towards Campiglia Marittima where the pioneering Jacopo Banti (tel: 0565 838802; www.jacopobanti.it) winery is located. Founded in 1931, this was the first to bottle wine in the Val di Cornia region, but it, along with other local wineries like Le Volpaiole (tel: 0565 843194) and Rigoli (tel: 0565 843079), doesn't make the most of some well-flavoured grapes.

From Campiglia Marittima head to the port of Piombino where the pick of the dry red wines is the Cabernets Franc and Sauvignon blend "Fidenzio" from Anna and Elio Tomomei's Podere San Luigi (info@poderesanluigi.li.it), although several of the smaller producers here produce highly charged olive oils and sweet Aleatico *passiti* reds.

Getting to Elba
Elba's tiny aerodrome (tel: 0565 976011) at La Pila in the middle of the island is served by both charter and scheduled flights from mainland Italy and some other European airports. However, most visitors arrive here by ferry. Ferries run from Piombino on the Italian mainland, and go mainly to Portoferraio (the crossing takes around one hour), but also to Rio Marina, Marina di Campo, and Porto Azzurro. Contact Moby Lines (tel: 0565 225211; www.mobylines.it) for car ferries and Toremar (tel: 0565 918080; www.toremar-elba.it) for car ferries and a quicker hovercraft link. Book well ahead in August.

Route Two: Elba

You can arrive on Elba from the mainland by ferry at Porto Azzurro. Take the main road out of town to Portoferraio and the first winery you come across is Mola (see box, right) at Gelsarello, where you can taste daily except Sundays (if you want a tour of the winery you must book ahead). This is a good place to acquaint yourself with Elba's Aleatico *passito*, a

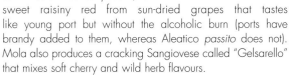

sweet raisiny red from sun-dried grapes that tastes like young port but without the alcoholic burn (ports have brandy added to them, whereas Aleatico *passito* does not). Mola also produces a cracking Sangiovese called "Gelsarello" that mixes soft cherry and wild herb flavours.

Next stop on the way to Portoferraio is Italo Sapere's Sapereta (see box, right; tours daily). The vineyards and olive groves here are organic, and the winery has a small and informative wine museum – Italo's grandparents founded the estate in 1927. There are also 17 independent agritourism apartments to rent. Sapereta's top red, "Vigna Thea", has the weighty fruit of old Sangiovese vines and the peppery panache of young Syrah ones. The Aleatico *passito* has beautifully clear wild black fruit served with a sprig of mint.

ABOVE *One of Bolgheri's most down-to-earth winemakers.*

Around Acquabona

Continue towards Portoferraio for Acquabona (see box, right; closed Sunday), signed on the right-hand side. The estate takes its name from the natural springs in the surrounding hills. The dry white wines here from Procanico (Trebbiano) are some of the island's best, but again the star attraction is the Aleatico *passito* for its insistent texture and bright fruit. The grapes are sun-dried in greenhouses.

If you want a break from wine, head to the nearby Acquabona golf club near Acquabona (tel: 0565 940066), which is open all year round and has a swimming pool and a bar. If not, follow signs to Elba's airport via the hamlet of Procchio for Cecilia (see box, right; open daily). The vineyards here are flatter than on most of the rest of the island, so owner Giuseppe Camerini buys in some grapes from more complex sites. He makes notably intense wines, including mouth-watering Aleatico *passito* and barrel-aged dry white and red wines in which any wood flavours are less obtrusive than the pink paint adorning his winery. From here head back to Porto Azzurro via the sleepy hamlet of Lacona.

WHERE TO STAY ON ELBA

Hotel Acquamarina [B4]
Loc Padulella
57037 Portoferraio (LI)
Tel: 0565 914057
www.hotelacquamarina.it
Close to the beach. Ask for a room with a terrace. Expensive.

WINERIES ON ELBA

Acquabona [A4]
Loc Acquabona, 1
57037 Portoferraio (LI)
Tel: 0565 933013
acquabona.elba@tiscalinet.it

Cecilia [A4]
La Casina, Loc La Pila
57034 Campo nell'Elba (LI)
Tel: 0565 977322

Mola [A3]
Loc Gelsarello, 2
57031 Porto Azzurro (LI)
Tel: 0565 958151
pavoletti@infol.it

Sapereta [A3]
Loc Mola
Via Provinciale Ovest, 73
57036 Porto Azzurro (LI)
Tel: 0565 95033
www.sapereonline.it

Grosseto and the Maremma

I t's worth taking your time getting to know Grosseto province in southern Tuscany. As well as half a dozen wine regions to visit, with the trendy Sangiovese or Morellino red of Scansano, there is the stunning town of Pitigliano looming out of volcanic rock. Both landlubbers and beach bums will find plenty to keep them busy.

LOCAL INFORMATION

Associazione Strada del Vino Colli di Maremma [B1]
Piazza Garibaldi, 51
58017 Pitigliano (GR)
Tel: 0564 617111
collidimaremma@tin.it
www.collidimaremma.it
Produces a good wine route map for the Morellino di Scansano, Bianco di Pitigliano, Parrina, Ansonica Costa dell'Argentario, Capalbio, and Sovana zones.

Associazione Strada del Vino Montecucco [C2]
Piazzale Cap Bruchi, 3
58044 Cinigiano (GR)
Tel: 0564 994630
info@stradadelvino
montecucco.it
www.stradadelvino
montecucco.it
Provides free maps of the Montecucco region and its wineries.

Strada del Vino Monteregio di Massa Marittima [D4]
Via Norma Parenti, 10
58024 Massa
Marittima (GR)
Tel: 0566 902756
stravin@cometanet.it
Provides free maps of the Monteregio di Massa Marittima region and its wineries.

The Grosseto coast has some fine sandy beaches around the Monte Argentario promontory – if you visit out of season the crowds diminish substantially; inland there are hot waterfall springs at Saturnia to cleanse your skin; or you can see the rich wildlife and migratory birds in the beautiful pine-studded Parco Regionale della Maremma which runs all along the coast.

The most famous wine of Grosseto is Morellino di Scansano, a Sangiovese red that became trendy in the last 10 to 15 years as outside investors from Chianti (Tenuta Sette Ponti), Montalcino (Biondi-Santi and Corte Pavone), and San Gimignano (Bruna Baroncini) planted vines in the hope of making softer reds than their own. Few have built wineries here so, for visits, concentrate on local producers who a) can receive you and b) generally have much older vines and make more consistent, if not always cheaper, wines than the interlopers.

Trebbiano takes centre stage

Another emerging region is Monteregio di Massa Marittima, source of Sangiovese-based reds and interesting dry whites based on the usually reviled Trebbiano, here made more flavourful by the blending in of Vermentino or the local Ansonica. This lemon-and-lime-flavoured white grape gets its own zone on terraced vineyards around the Costa dell'Argentario, whose resorts of Porto Santo Stefano and Porto Ercole provide the seafood with which this white goes best. More minor zones around Monte Argentario, a "mountain" promontory now joined to the coast by silting, include Parrina with its traditionally run winery La Parrina, and Capalbio.

Inland regions include Montecucco, which overlooks Montalcino to the north and where a range of altitudes and exposures to the sun helps create potentially complex red and white blends; Sovana, where Sangiovese-dominated vineyards surround some fine Etruscan sites which you can visit; and Pitigliano, arguably the most stunning-looking of all Tuscan wine towns, and home to dry, tingly whites made from Sauvignon Blanc and Chardonnay blended onto a Trebbiano base. Look out, too, for wines labelled with the

Maremma or Tuscan IGT designations – they can be some of
the best value in Tuscany.

Getting there

Bus services throughout Grosseto province are operated by
Rama (www.griforama.it), whose main hub is near the railway
station in Grosseto town. Trains from Grosseto are on the main
Rome–Livorno coastal train line. Via Aurelia, the Rome–Livorno
road, bypasses Grosseto, with Rome 300km (187 miles) to the
south, and Livorno 100km (62 miles) to the north.

Travelling around

Route summaries There are three possible itineraries here.
Route One summary From Grosseto to Paganico, Sasso
d'Ombrone, Montecucco, Cinigiano,
Casteldelpiano, and Montenero.
Then back to Grosseto via
Paganico. Total distance
200km (125 miles).
Allow one or
two days.

Route One: Montecucco
Allow one or two days

Route Two: Monteregio
di Massa Marittima
Allow one or two days

Route Three: Southern Grosseto
Allow one or two days

The Etruscan coast

Grosetto

WINERIES IN GROSSETO

In Montecucco:

Azienda Le Vigne [D2]
58040 Montenero
d'Orcia (GR)
Tel: 0564 954116
info@aziendalevigne.com
www.aziendalevigne.com

Orciaverde [D2]
Montenero d'Orcia (GR)
Tel: 0564 954112
orciaverde@virgilio.it

Salustri [D2]
Loc La Cava
Poggi del Sasso
58040 Cinigiano (GR)
Tel: 0564 990529
info@salustri.it
www.salustri.it

*In Monteregio di
Massa Marittima:*

Massa Vecchia [D4]
Loc Massa Vecchia
58024 Massa
Marittima (GR)
Tel: 0566 904144
massavecchia@inwind.it

Morisfarms [D4]
Loc Curanuova
Fattoria Poggetti
58024 Massa
Marittima (GR)
Tel: 0566 919135
morisfarms@morisfarms.it
www.morisfarms.it

Nannoni Grappa [D3]
Fattoria Aratrice
58100 Paganico (GR)
Tel: 0564 905204
nannonisas@libero.it

Serraiola [E4]
Fraz Frassine
Loc Serraiola
58025 Monterotondo
Marittimo (GR)
Tel: 0566 910026
info@serraiola.it

Route Two summary From Grosseto town to Roccastrada, Massa Marittima, Monterotondo Marittimo, and Scarlino then back to Grosseto. Total distance 200km (125 miles). Allow one or two days.

Route Three summary From Grosseto town to Scansano, Magliano in Toscana, Parrina, Orbetello, Capalbio, Manciano, Pitigliano, Sovana, Saturnia, Scansano, and back to Grosseto. Total distance 285km (177 miles). Allow one or two days.

Route One: Montecucco

From Grosseto take the SS223 through Paganico and turn right after the town to Sasso d'Ombrone. Bear right for the hamlet of Poggi del Sasso for Salustri (*see* box, left). Leonardo Salustri and his son Marco have a smart tasting room/office, and produce the most attractive range of red wines in the Montecucco zone. The early-ripening Merlot is planted on cooler, north-facing sites to, as Leonardo says, "make it work harder for its ripeness, and give more complex flavours". Most of the budwood for the Sangiovese vines here has been propagated by hand by the Salustris, with plants capable of producing small berries that are rich in colour and flavour. Salustri's reds have so much elegance and purity you wonder where they find the time to keep a flock of sheep and farm wheat, too. There are also seven self-catering apartments, plus a pool, and great views of the high Maremma hills.

Also in Poggi del Sasso is the huge Castello Colle Massari winery (tel: 0564 990498), part-owned by the wealthy Claudio Tipa of Podere Grattamacco in Bolgheri (*see* p.128). Once complete, this winery will have modern visitor facilities and be the largest winery in the Montecucco zone.

Going to market

Continue to Montecucco winery (www.tenutadimontecucco.it) whose wine style for both red and white is still very much evolving. This is the historic heart of the Montecucco zone, the Montecucco estate having been created out of a medieval *borgo* or fortified hamlet with its own chapel.

Turn right onto the SP113 just before the row of cypress leading to the Montecucco estate to access Cinigiano whose weekly market (Tuesdays) features seasonal produce. Continue over a mix of soft hills and sharp turns via the village of Monticello to reach the outskirts of Casteldelpiano which has lots of (now largely disused) underground wine cellars. As Montecucco's reputation grows as a wine producer, these may come back into use. This is the highest part of the Montecucco zone, so bring snow chains if visiting wineries in winter.

Head down towards the Orcia and Ombrone rivers past the hamlet of Montegiovi, which sits on a rocky outcrop like ice-

cream does on a cone, turning right at Casalino hamlet for Azienda Le Vigne (*see* box, left; book ahead for tours in English). Owners Chiara and Andrea Pettini produce cereals and olives as well as vines, but sensibly the vines here are grown on the rockiest, harshest terrain. Sangiovese, Merlot, and experimental 100% Ciliegiolo reds show real promise, especially since the Pettinis only began vinifying their own grapes from 2002.

Drop down towards the valley floor past Montenero hamlet where Allesandro Bocci's emerging Perazzeta (www.perazzeta.it) winery is found; a source of decent dry white wine from mainly Trebbiano filled out by one-third Chardonnay and Malvasia. Also here is the hugely committed Dario Pasqui's Trottolo estate (tel: 0564 954125; trottolowine@libero.it). A windy, well-exposed site makes for crisp, insistent reds, with the necessary substance for barrel-ageing in the case of the *riservas*.

ABOVE *The countryside is dotted with fortified towns and farms, a legacy from medieval times.*

Added altitude

Further towards Paganico is Simone and Manuela Governi's Orciaverde (*see* box, left). There are just two hectares of vines here, including some old-vine Ciliegiolo for extra richness, a barrel cellar located in an old water tower, and Chianina cows bred for their meat. The Governis also rent vines in Cinigiano, the higher altitude there giving the reds extra zip. The wines are marked by lush fruit overlaid with toasty oak.

One more estate worthy of mention on the way back to Grosseto (right hand side past the turn to Montalcino) is Duilio

RIGHT *Umbrella pines provide shade on Tuscany's coastal roads.*

and Luciana Sodi's Parmoleto. There are four apartments here to rent (18 beds), too. You can self-cater, or eat with the owners whose modesty matches their red wines' natural reserve.

Route Two: Monteregio di Massa Marittima
From Grosseto take the old road (not the SS1 Aurelia) to Montepescali for the SS73 to Roccastrada. The grappa specialist Nannoni (see p.134; by prior appointment) is located at Fattoria dell'Aratrice between Roccastrada and Paganico. Grappa is made by distilling the liquid residue from fermented grape skins (le vinacce). Gioacchino Nannoni was the first in Tuscany to produce grappa di fattoria, in other words distilling grappas from individual estates. Nannoni distils only from the best vinacce taken from wineries like Sassicaia, Montevertine, and Mantellassi. The best time to visit is around harvest time, as this is when the stills are working.

From Roccastrada head towards Massa Marittima via the hamlets of Montemassi and Ribolla. In Ribolla you'll pass Carlo Falciani's emerging I Campetti (icampetti@virgilio.it), source of interesting Malvasia and Viognier whites and approachable Cabernet, Merlot, Sangiovese, and Colorino reds.

Turn right off the Ribolla–Follonica road to Massa Marittima just after Marta Matteini and Marco Querci's Campo Bargello (www.campobargello.it), where you can rent four independent apartments (10 beds) surrounded by olive groves and woodland teeming with pheasants, porcupines, and deer.

Flattened out
The landscape flattens towards Massa Marittima, and as the land rises on the south side of the town off the Follonica–Siena road you'll find Fabrizio and Patrizia Niccolaini's Massa Vecchia (see p.134). This estate encapsulates everything that is good about Tuscan wine: vineyards ploughed by a pair of Maremma cows (one of which always insists on standing on the left-hand side!); organically farmed old vines with super-low yields and minimal spraying; Livornese chickens (a rare breed) running wild in the olive groves; new vineyards being trained up fruit trees (instead of along wires) like the ancient Etruscans did; and wines of

incredible complexity, concentration, freshness, and depth. The red Poggi a'Venti knocks so-called Super Tuscans like Ornellaia into a cocked hat with its wild fruit flavours. Dry Vermentino whites and Aleatico *passito* are mouth-filling. If you book ahead you can buy wine in bulk which is cheaper than buying in bottle. The owners will tell you how best to store the wine, too.

A feast of Sangiovese

Now head north to Monterotondo Marittima, then west towards Suvereto (*see* Etruscan Coast chapter) in the Val di Cornia. Just past Frassine you'll find Serraiola (*see* p.134), a mixed farm notable for buttery dry white wines from Viognier and Chardonnay, plus easily quaffed Sangiovese reds like "Lentisco" and "Cervone".

The next winery towards Suvereto is the Camerini brothers' Suveraia (*see* box, left), whose energetic, unfiltered Sangiovese "Rosso di Campetroso" is the star attraction. Head back to Grosseto via the Riserva Naturale Tre Cancelli. Just before you join the SS1 Roma–Livorno road you'll see Morisfarms signposted (*see* p.134). The Moris family (their name recalls a medieval Moorish incursion here) produces a range of juicy, modern-style reds like "Avvoltore", from a Sangiovese, Cabernet, and Syrah vineyard that you can see from the Via Aurelia. There is a herd of (domesticated) wild boar, plus extensive woodland.

Our route heads back to Grosseto on the Via Aurelia, or take the more scenic coastal route through two nature reserves, the Poggio Spedaletto and the Diaccia Botrona.

WHERE TO STAY

Antico Casale di Scansano [B2] Loc Castagneta
58054 Scansano (GR)
Tel: 0564 507219
www.anticocasale
discansano.com
Unpretentious, child-friendly hotel. Reliable restaurant. Sign up for trekking, cooking courses or riding lessons.

Le Calle [D3]
Loc La Cava
58040 Poggi del Sasso (GR)
Tel: 0564 990432
www.le-calle.it
Three apartments plus pool on peaceful organic farm with Amiatino donkeys, sheep, organic vines, and olives.

Podere Vignone [D2]
58038 Vignone (GR)
Tel: 0564 950569
Great views across organic olive groves to Mount Amiata. Short walk from the hamlet of Seggiano, home to a lively olive oil festival every December 26.

I Poggetti [E4]
Loc Curanuova
58024 Massa Marittima (GR)
Tel: 0564 996626
www.villeinmaremma.com
Peaceful modern villas and farmhouses suitable for families, plus pool.

San Guglielmo [D3]
Loc Venturi
58036 Roccastrada (GR)
Tel: 0564 577581
Simple stone house with six well-equipped bedrooms, not far from the sea.

Sant'Anna [C2]
58044 Cinigiano (GR)
Tel: 0564 993559
www.agrisantanna.com
Two apartments plus pool and restaurant serving juicy home-reared lamb, super stews, and cherry cakes.

ABOVE *Vines tied down in anticipation of summer growth.*

Route Three: Southern Grosseto

Leave Grosseto on the SP159 road to Campagnatico but turn right to cross the Ombrone to enter the Morellino di Scansano zone at Istia d'Ombrone. Immediately Le Pupille (see p.136) is signed (also under the name of its owner, Elisabetta Geppetti). The cellars here date from 2001, with the vaulted barrel rooms at ground floor level due to the high water table. The vineyards are well sited, both here and in other locations in the Morellino zone. Geppetti's most classic red comes from her oldest vineyard, Saffredi, and is made from Cabernet, Merlot, and Grenache Noir (here called Alicante).

If you follow the Ombrone northeast to Arcille you'll find Poggio TreValle (see p.136), one of the most traditional wineries in the Scansano zone. Brothers Umberto and Bernardo Valle came here from southern Italy in the 1990s and now make two unfiltered Morellino di Scansanos called "Larcille" and "Fròndina" from organic grapes. Both offer soft flavours of earth and wild hedgerow fruit mixed with the graininess older barrels can bring. You'll find the wines in local restaurants.

Stay on the SP159 to Scansano for Giancarlo Lanza and Giulia Andreozzi's friendly I Botri and the rather dull Scansano co-op.

Sun, stone, and super-ripe grapes

Get on the SP160 which has some great views towards Magliano in Toscana and stop in the hamlet of Impostino for Mantellassi (see p.136; English spoken; open daily). This was a mixed farm with sheep and cows until recently, but the success of the Mantellassi family's wines means they now concentrate on their vineyards. On your way up the long unsurfaced road to the winery you can see large stones between the vines which retain the sun's heat and make for super-ripe grapes. Mantellassi produces generously lush Morellino di Scansano plus the unusual "Querciolaia", a tarry red with vanilla flavours from barrel-ageing made from old Grenache vines (here called Alicante as it was probably introduced by medieval seafarers from that part of Spain). Mantellassi's dry white "Lucamone" is one of the Tuscan coast's most dynamic Vermentino wines.

Past Magliano in Toscana turn right onto the SP81 which goes to the Via Aurelia, passing La Selva (see p.136) on the way. The ebullient Bavarian Karl Egger founded La Selva after he came to Tuscany to become a small-scale "gentleman farmer" after a successful career in electronics. He now has a vast farm producing fruit, grain, and vegetables as well as an organic vineyard. The winery shop has a huge range of Egger's food products such as olive paste, pickled chillies, aubergines in vinegar, and artichoke cream, all fairly priced. Delicious dry white Vermentino, soft Morellino di Scansanos, plus a solidly prune-like varietal Ciliegiolo called "Colli dell'Uccellina" (or "bird hill") are the stand-outs. Visits to the winery run until 5pm every Wednesday, with a small fee to cover wine tasting.

Historic hound
From La Selva take the Via Aurelia south towards Rome. On the left, Tenuta La Parrina (www.tuscany.net/parrina) is signposted at the town of Albinia. The estate is full of history – the threshing machine was invented here, and the white Maremma sheepdog was first bred here, too. La Parrina's comfortable accommodation is good for families as there is a restaurant on site. Many crops are grown, including peaches, apples, kiwis, vegetables, and vines. The coast is so close that frost is rare, making crop levels steady. The atmospheric shop is a grocery, dairy counter, and wine store rolled into one, selling the estate's sheep's and goats' cheeses, yoghurt, conserves, sauces, balsamic vinegar, honey, olive oil, and wine. La Parrina makes weighty dry whites under the Ansonica Costa dell'Argentario, Parrina Bianco, and Capalbio Bianco designations. Red Morellino di Scansano and Parrina Rosso are consistently attractive, with new oak in the background, allowing the grape flavours to shine.

Back on the Via Aurelia heading south at Orbetello Scalo turn right for the Monte Argentario peninsula and Danei (see p.136; by appointment only). Owner Nunzio Danei can be a hard man to track down, but if you can find a bottle of his sweet Ansonica passito you'll see why this style of wine is called a "meditation wine" by Italians; as you ponder how so many citrus and tropical fruit flavours can be crammed into just one wine.

See what's on the cards
Continue south on the Via Aurelia until you see the SP63 Capalbio road. You pass the co-op (www.cantinacapalbio.it) on the way, but you'll have more fun here by visiting the Giardino dei Tarocchi or "Tarot Gardens" in Garavicchio (tel: 0564 895122). It is open in the afternoons from mid-May to the end of October, but book ahead if you can. The gardens are located in an old quarry and show the Tarot figures in such a way that you can climb into, or onto, the sculptures.

From Capalbio access the SP75 (east) to get on the SP101 direction Manciano, where the leading winery Acquaviva (tel: 0564 602890; fattoria@relaidvillaacquaviva.com) offers a Morellino di Scansano and a pretty agritourism farmhouse. From Manciano take the SP74 to Pitigliano, travelling through

WHERE TO EAT

Antica Trattoria Aurora [B3]
Via Chiasso Lavagnini, 12/14
58051 Magliano
in Toscana (GR)
Tel: 0564 592030
Duck with ravioli filled with onion and roast pigeon. Closed Wednesday.

Canapone Wine Bar [C3]
Piazza Alighieri, 3
58100 Grosseto (GR)
Tel: 0564 24546
Great value fried and grilled fish, with value wines, too.

Osteria da Tronca [D4]
Vicolo Porte, 5
58024 Massa Marittima (GR)
Tel: 0566 901991
Closed Wednesday. Wild asparagus (in season), tripe, roast rabbit with garlic and rosemary, plus salt cod.

La Posta [C2]
58040 Cinigiano (GR)
Tel: 0564 993430
Unprepossessing menu disguising intense, hot appetisers, plus fresh seafood pasta and generous pizzas.

Ristorante La Chimera [C3]
Via Batignanese, 206
Roselle Terme (GR)
Tel: 0564 402112
Fish only. Octopus, seafood salad, clam spaghetti. Book ahead. Closed Mondays and Tuesday lunchtimes.

Taverna di Campagna [C3]
Via Firenze, 10
58030 Monte Antico (GR)
Tel: 0564 991030
Maremma cooking, with huge spinach and ricotta ravioli and even bigger pizzas.

Taverna del Vecchio Borgo [D4] Via N. Parenti, 12
58024 Massa Marittima (GR)
Tel: 0566 903950
Closed Sunday and Monday.

twisting gorges until the town appears above you. The Jewish quarter, *La Piccola Jerusalemme*, dates from 1598, and has been restored for visitors. The local co-op makes a kosher wine, found in the town's wine shops.

Around Sovana

To reach Carla Benini and Eduardo Ventimiglia's excellent Sassotondo (*see* p.136) from Pitigliano look for the SP46 to Sovana before you enter the town. The electric fence running around the certified organic vineyard keeps wild boar out. The cavernous winery is cut into tufa rock, keeping temperatures constant, good for maintaining steady fermentations, and thus flavours in the wine. You can feel this in Sassotondo's grassy dry white wines, which are made from Greco, Chardonnay, Trebbiano, and Sauvignon Blanc. Red wines from Sangiovese, Ciliegiolo, and Alicante (Grenache Noir) show the rich glycerol softness that comes from old vines.

A few kilometres after Sovana on the SP46 at San Martino sul Fiora is La Busattina (*see* p.136). Emilio and Elisabetta Falcione's estate affords stunning views across the Maremma. Rare breeds of farm animals are kept here, such as Amiatino donkeys and Montecristo goats, great for children. The wines are made in a tiny cellar under the farmhouse. The first wine (always unfiltered) was made in 2000, but the Falciones already produce a deliciously crisp range of citrussy Sovana DOC whites and Sovana Superiore reds full of red berry flavours. Herbal teas are used on the vineyards, with common horsetail used to prevent mildew – "it saved our crop in 2004," says Emilio.

At the crossroads take the SP10 towards Manciano via Saturnia, then the SP159 to Scansano and back to Grosseto.

RIGHT *Tuscany is the perfect place to get away from the daily grind.*

INDEX